THE WARRIOR KŌANS

Trevor Leggett originally studied law at King's College, London, but has spent most of his working life as Head of the Japanese Service of the BBC. He has studied Judo to a very high level and taught the art in the UK for several years, founding a Judo club in North London. In 1984 he was awarded the Order of the Sacred Treasure by the Japanese Government, for services in spreading Japanese culture abroad – a rare honour for a non-Japanese. He retired in 1970, but still broadcasts as a guest in Japanese on the BBC's transmissions to Japan. He is the author of several books on Zen Buddhism including *Zen and the Ways*, *The Tiger's Cave* and *Encounters in Yoga and Zen* (all published by Routledge & Kegan Paul).

絵
47

吾家話頭
典據乎水
莫如猫兒
問取狗子

黒田氏長政公於予如是評爲
鳴呼吾老圓而頗寫怪偶一地
寄其白菅地
八十二歳老衲書屋雪圏

古斗室少膳

A very unusual picture of an interview in the fourteenth
century between the feudal lord Kuroda and a Zen master on
the kōan 'Is there Buddha nature in the dog?' 'No'.

THE WARRIOR KŌANS
Early Zen in Japan

Trevor Leggett

ARKANA

London, Boston and Henley

To the late Dr Hari Prasad Shastri
these translations are reverently dedicated

First published in 1985 by Arkana, an imprint of
Routledge & Kegan Paul plc

14 Leicester Square, London WC2H 7PH, England

9 Park Street, Boston, Mass. 02108, USA

Broadway House, Newtown Road,
Henley on Thames, Oxon RG9 1EN, England

Set in Sabon
by Hope Services Ltd, Abingdon
and printed in Great Britain
by The Guernsey Press Co Ltd,
Guernsey, Channel Islands

Library of Congress Cataloging in Publication Data

Leggett, Trevor.

The warrior kōans.
Includes index.
1. Shōnan Kattōroku. 2. Kōan—
Early works to 1800. I. Title.
BQ9289.L44 1985   294.3'85   85–6060

British Library CIP data also available

ISBN 1–85063–023–2

CONTENTS

Contents

Contents

Contents

PREFACE

The collection of 100 odd kōans here presented in translation was put together in 1545, under the name Shōnan Kattōroku, from records in the Kamakura temples dating back to the foundation of Kenchōji in 1253 when pure Zen first came to Japan. For a long time the teachers at Kamakura were mainly Chinese masters, who came in a stream for over a century. As a result, this Zen was conducted between masters and pupils not fluent in each other's language.

On the political and religious background, there are explanations in my book *Zen and the Ways,* in which I translated about one quarter of these kōans. In that book I gave some account of the then Rinzai system of kōan riddles, and the modifications that were introduced when this line of Zen came to Japan.

The text in its present form was reconstituted from fragmentary records in Kenchōji and other temples in Kamakura by Imai Fukuzan, a great scholar of Zen in the early part of this century. He was joint author, with Nakagawa Shūan, of a standard reference book of Zen phrases, *Zengo-jii.* Imai was himself a veteran Zen practitioner, as had been his father before him, and he knew personally many of the great figures of Zen at the end of the nineteenth and the first quarter of the twentieth century. In the small edition (500 copies) of the Shōnan Kattōroku collection which he published in 1925, he put a number of notes of his own, and I have translated most of these along with the kōans to which they refer. His Introduction to the text is put here at the beginning, along with extracts from his Introduction to a much longer work, to have been called *Warrior Zen*, of which this was to have been only the first part. That work was never completed, and much of the Introduction consists of long lists of Zen masters at the Imperial palace, with feudal lords, or teaching warriors in various parts of the country. However, there are some references to the present text, and these I have translated, along with a few personal details which he gives. Imai was one of the few scholars who studied Zen at the time, and the last to examine in depth the Kenchōji records before they were almost entirely destroyed in the earthquake in 1924. His studies are therefore of great interest and importance for the history of Zen in Japan.

Imai's book is now rare. Inouye Tetsujirō republished it as one item in volume 7 of his *Bushidō Zenshū*, in 1942; this is also now rare. Inouye added a few notes of his own, which I have occasionally translated.

Many of the samurai whose interviews are recorded here were what was called *Nyūdō* (entering the Way), which meant that they had taken Buddhist vows and shaved their heads, though without leaving their families as a priest had to do. According to Imai's researches, there were 365 names of warriors listed in the Kamakura records as having taken these vows, but Zen interviews are recorded of only 172.

There are a number of kōan interviews with women recorded, mostly but not entirely from the warrior class. The samurai women were famous for their strength of character, and for moral strictness. The women teachers developed a number of kōans of their own (see for instance No. 30).

The warrior pupils of the early period of Kamakura Zen had no bent for scholarship and could not be taught by means of the classical kōans from the Chinese records of the patriarchs. The Zen teachers of the time trained them by making up kōans on the spot, in what came to be called shikin Zen or on-the-instant Zen. Zen master Daikaku's One-robe

Zen (No. 6) and its variant, Bukkō's Loincloth Zen, are examples.

When the Chinese master Daikaku first came to Japan in 1246, neither he nor his Japanese samurai pupils could speak the other's language, and there are many instances in old accounts of the difficulties he had in communicating. For instance, in an old record in Kenchōji there is a passage describing an interview between him and Toyama, Lord of Tango, and in it comes the phrase Maku-maa-sun, maku-maa-sun, nyu-su-kū-ri-i-fu-ya. This was Daikaku's Sung dynasty Chinese taken down phonetically by a scribe who did not understand it. The priest Ki Zentoku, a man of Szechuan who had come with Shōichi to Kamakura, transliterated this into the proper Chinese characters, which a Japanese scholar could then read as Maku-mō-zō, maku-mō-zō, ji-ze-gan-rai-butsu-ya, and Endō Moritsugu, who could read Chinese, translated it into Japanese: 'No delusive thoughts, no delusive thoughts! Surely you are yourself from the very beginning Buddha!' Many such cases are reported where what was said by a Chinese Zen master was transcribed into Chinese characters and then translated into Japanese by a Japanese scholar of Chinese. (We can see that often the phrase is repeated by the Chinese, a characteristic found even today.) In these cases the translation was then passed to the Japanese Zen pupil.

Then there were also those who, in the early days, took their Zen interviews with the Chinese master by means of writing with a brush. (Japanese of some literary attainments could read and write the Chinese characters in the Chinese order, but they did not pronounce them as the Chinese did, nor recognize them so pronounced. In the same way today, a mathematical calculation could be written by an Englishman and understood by a Russian even though neither of them could recognize the figures when read aloud by the other.)

Again, sometimes Ki Zentoku acted as an interpreter at the interview.

But the main point was, that the teachers had mostly only a very limited knowledge of Japanese, which meant that the style of this Zen did not admit of many words, and classical kōans like those of the Hekiganshū or Kattōshū could scarcely be appropriate for bringing warriors under the hammer, as it is called in Zen. It is stated clearly in the Kyōchū Zakki (Jottings from the Ravine), the diary of priest Giō, that Daikaku used to make up on-the-spot kōans suited to that particular pupil. This was the shikin Zen, or on-the-instant Zen. The fact that in the hundred kōans of this collection there are so few which derive from Chinese T'ang or Sung kōans bears out Giō's statement.

Again, in regard to the 'comment' (agyo) which the pupils had to produce to meet some of the tests, the situation was not that in the Takuju or Inzan schools today, where sometimes in order to pass, a particular phrase has to be presented (often from the Zenrin Kushū collection of Zen sayings, put together by the Japanese for just this purpose). In those early days provided it was an expression of genuine realization, a poem or a song or (somewhat later) a line from the Nō drama would be acceptable without question. Imai remarks that a collection existed of the agyo comments which had been passed by teachers of the great Kamakura Zen temples; as a seasoned Zen man himself as well as a historian, he was permitted to see it, and he says that it contains many poems and lines from the Nō dramas, besides the well-known Zenrin Kushū quotations which later became *de rigueur*. He says that this collection had never been made public, but he does give one example. When Hōjō Tokiyori, the Regent, was taking under Master Gottan the classical kōan 'The Tree in the Forecourt' he presented the poem:

If we split open the cherry tree
    We find no flower there;
It is the spring that becomes the seed of the blossoms.

This was translated and accepted by Master Gottan. Imai

adds that this gives a good idea of the old Kamakura Zen.

It is interesting that this poem precedes by over a century the famous verse attributed to Ikkyū, when he was challenged by a swordsman to produce the Buddha-nature. He replied that it is 'in the breast of man', and the opponent drew his sword to 'cut the breast open to find it'. Ikkyū made the verse:

The cherry-blossoms of Yoshino, which will bloom with the
    spring –
If we cut the tree open to find them, where would they be?

A number of these kōan stories make reference to the Katzu! shout, with occasional reference to a power of using it to strike a man unconscious. This is a field in which emotional scepticism is as strong as emotional credulity. It may be noted that in these records the victims were in many cases professional fighters. For a relatively modern instance, see E.J. Harrison's *The fighting spirit of Japan* (Foulsham). Harrison was a famous journalist in the Far East at the beginning of the century, who was also a considerable scholar, having a good knowledge of Japanese, of Russian, and even of that curiosity among languages, Lithuanian. In his youth however, he had been round the world in search of adventure, becoming for a time a lumberjack. He became an expert at Jūjutsu, and then at Jūdō. In his early days he was a compulsive bar-room fighter; there are accounts of some of his exploits in memoirs of old hands in Japan, such as Martyr. He had to give this up when he took up Jūdō, but he remained one of the most aggressive men I have ever met. He would not have been easy to overawe or 'hypnotize', especially in the pride of youth. Nevertheless he found himself helpless before an old Japanese expert of the warrior shout.

Imai's comments reflect accurately the distinction between the Zen shout and that practised by the warriors.

ACKNOWLEDGMENTS

I am grateful to Sōfukuji temple for permission to reproduce the unusual picture of the Mu kōan, and to Kamakura Museum for several of the pictures of early Zen figures. Professor Hajime Nakamura has taken a kindly interest in this book, and Mrs M. Fujimoto and the Tokyo Shoseki Company were most generous in arranging for the printing of the index.

IMAI FUKUZAN'S INTRODUCTION TO SHŌNANKATTŌROKU

The origin of warrior Zen in Kamakura, and in the whole of the eastern part of Japan, goes back to the training of warrior pupils by Eisai (Senkō Kokushi). But it was the training of warriors and priests by two great Chinese masters, Daikaku and Bukkō, which became the Zen style of the Kamakura temples. There were three streams in Kamakura Zen:

> scriptural Zen;
> on-the-instant (shikin) Zen;
> Zen adapted to the pupil (ki-en Zen).

Scriptural Zen derives from Eisai, founder of Jufukuji in Kamakura in 1215, and of Kenninji in Kyōto. But at that time it was rare to find in Kamakura any samurai who had literary attainments, so that the classical kōans from Chinese records of patriarchs could hardly be given to them. The teacher therefore selected passages from various sūtras for the warriors, and for monks also. These specially devised scriptural Zen kōans used by Eisai at Kamakura numbered only eighteen, and so the commentary to the Sōrinzakki calls Jufukuji 'temple of the eighteen diamond kōans'. However, after Eisai, his successors in Kamakura of the Ōryū line (to which he belonged – the founder died in China in 1069 and the line was dying out there when it was brought across by Eisai) soon brought them up to one hundred scriptural kōans, to meet the various temperaments and attainments of their pupils. These successors were Gyōyū, Zōsō, and Jakuan at

1

Jufukuji; Daiei, Kohō, Myōō at Zenkōji; Sozan, Gakkō at Manjuji, and others.

Among these augmented scriptural kōans were passages from the sūtras but also from the sayings of the patriarchs, to suit the depth or shallowness of comprehension of pupils, whether monks or laymen. Thus the warriors who applied for Zen training in Kamakura in the early days studied both the Buddha Zen (nyorai Zen) and the patriarchal Zen, but it can be said that those who were given classical kōans from the Hekiganshū or Mumonkan and so on would have been extremely few. From the end of the sixteenth century, however, the teachers did begin to rely mainly on stories from the records of the patriarchs, for training both monks and laymen. Kamakura Zen now gradually deteriorated, and by about 1630 no printed text of the Shōnankattōroku existed, but only manuscript copies. Some time towards the end of the seventeenth century, a priest named Tōan in Izumi selected ninety-five of the (Kamakura) scriptural kōans, and got a friend, a priest named Sōji, to have them printed as a two-volume work entitled Kyōjōkōanshū (anthology of scriptural kōans). These ninety-five correspond to the Kamakura scriptural kōans, though with five missing (two from the Diamond Sūtra, one from the Kegon Sūtra, one from the Lotus Sūtra and one from the Heart Sūtra). This book still existed in 1925.

On-the-instant Zen (shikin-Zen, sometimes read sokkon-Zen) arose from the training of warriors by Daikaku, first teacher at Kenchōji. He had come to Japan in 1246, and had been briefly at Enkakuji of Hakata city in Kyūshū, and then at Kyōto; while his Japanese was still imperfect, and without taking time to improve it, he came to Kamakura. Thus this teacher had to be sparing of words, and in training pupils he did not present them with classical kōans about Chinese patriarchs which would have required long explanations of the history and circumstances of the foreign country; instead he made kōans then and there on the instant, and set them to

2

the warriors as a means to give them the essential first glimpse. Bukkō Kokushi, founder of Enkakuji, arriving in Japan on the last day of the sixth month of 1280, came to Kamakura in the autumn of the same year, so that he too had no time to learn Japanese but began meeting people straight away. He also had to confine himself to speaking only as necessary, and in the same way made kōans for his warrior pupils on the spur of the moment. Thus at both these great temples there was what was called 'shikin' or on-the-instant Zen. Before Daikaku came to Japan, something of the true patriarchal Zen had been introduced by such great Zen figures as Dōgen and Shōichi (Bennen), but monks and laymen were mostly not equal to it and many missed the main point in a maze of words and phrases. Consequently Bukkō finally gave up the use of classical kōans for Zen aspirants who came to him in Kamakura, and made them absorb themselves in things directly concerning them. The Regent Tokimune himself was one of the early pupils in this on-the-instant Zen, and he was one who grasped its essence.

Zen adapted to the pupil meant, at Kamakura, making a kōan out of some incident or circumstance with which a monk or layman was familiar, and putting test questions (satsumon) to wrestle with. It would have been very difficult for the Kamakura warriors, with their little learning, to throw themselves at the outset right into the old kōan incidents in the records of the patriarchs. So in the Zen temples of Kamakura and of eastern Japan generally, the style was that only when their Zen had progressed somewhat did they come under the hammer of one of the classical kōans.

Among the old manuscript books in Kanazawa and Nirayama libraries there are many concerning Kamakura Zen, for instance Nyūdōsanzenki, Gosannyūdōshū and so on. But it is only the Shōnankattōroku which has a commentary with details of when each kōan began to be used as such, and in which temple, and also discourses and sermons on them.

In the tenth month of 1543, a great Zen convention was

held at Meigetsuin as part of the memorial service, on the 150th anniversary of the death of Lord Uesugi Norikata, its founder. Five hundred printed copies of the Shōnankattōroku were distributed to those attending. The book included sermons on the kōans by Muin, the rōshi of Zenkōji. The work consisted of a hundred kōan stories selected from Gosannyūdōshū and other texts, by Muin Rōshi, as particularly suited to the warriors whom he was training at the time. With the decline of Kamakura Zen at the end of the sixteenth century, the copies of this book disappeared and it became extremely difficult to find one. What remained in the temples were almost entirely manuscript copies.

In 1918 I examined the old records at Kenchōji in the four repositories of the sub-temples of Tengen, Ryūhō, Hōju and Sairai, and among the stacks of old books there were some seventeenth-century manuscript copies of the Shōnankattōroku, but all had pages missing from the ravages of worms, and it was barely possible to confirm from part of the contents that they had all been copies of one and the same book. In the first years of Meiji, Yamaoka Tesshū was given a copy by the Zen priest Shōjō of Ryūtaku temple in Izu, and he allowed Imai Kidō to make a further copy of it.

In this way I came into touch with a copy, but this was lent and re-lent, and finally became impossible to trace. There are some collections of notes of laymen who were set some of these kōans at Kamakura temples, but the teachers when they gave one did not say what number it was, and so in these notes the kōans are not tabulated. It was only after finding a list of contents in one of the Kenchōji manuscripts that I was able to determine the order of the full hundred kōans as recorded in the present work. In Kamakura Zen there were thirty other kōans used mainly by teachers of the Ōryū line (mostly at Jufukuji, Zenkōji, and Manjuji – temples traditionally connected with Eisai), which are from Bukedōshinshū (thirteenth volume at Zenkōji), Bushōsōdan (eleventh volume at Jufukuji), and Sōrinzakki (fifteenth volume at Kenchōji), but I have omitted these and present here only the hundred kōans of Shōnankattōroku.

Zen tests (sassho) differ with the teacher. Those given to those trained at Enkakuji in the Sōryūkutsu (blue dragon cave) interview room of Master Kōsen (one of the greatest Meiji rōshis) were exceptional tests, and again the tests set by Shunnō of Nanzenji, and the formidable Sekisōken tests were not the same. The teachers Keichū and Shinjō had tests of their own. The sassho included here have been taken from a collection of 460 Kamakura sassho recorded in the Tesshiroku (fourth volume in the manuscript copy). These of course have themselves been picked out from many different interviews with different pupils, but I believe they would have been tests devised by teachers when each kōan was first being set as such; so the collection will have come from something over a hundred different teachers. Of course sometimes a single teacher devised more than one kōan, but if we reckon that Kamakura teachers made 130 kōans, we can take it that the sassho tests devised at the initiation of the separate kōans would have come from over 100 teachers.

The Shōnankattōroku kōans had sermons and discourses with them as well as a note as to the origination of each one, but here only this last is included. The discourses and sermons are so full of old Kamakura words and expressions that annotations would come to be as long as the original text.

Some tests required a 'comment' (chakugo or jakugo). In general these are kept secret and not to be disclosed, but as an example I have included some of the comments on the Mirror Zen poems used at Tōkeiji.

At the end of the sixteenth century Kamakura Zen was gradually deteriorating, and when with the Tokugawa era the country entered a long period of peace, warriors were no longer required to confront the issue of life and death on the battlefield. And it was perhaps for this reason that the quality of those who entered Kamakura Zen was not heroic like that of the old warriors, and both priests and lay followers became fewer. Kamakura Zen begins with 'one word' and ends with absorption in 'one Katzu!' Its main kōan is the Katzu! and unless one could display Zen action at the turning-point of life and death, he was not passed through. Sometimes a naked sword was at the centre of the interview (in later centuries represented by a fan).

Kamakura Zen was for those who might be called upon to die at any moment, and both teacher and pupils had to have tremendous spirit. Today those who with their feeble power of meditation, casually entertain visions of passing through many kōans, cannot undertake it. In that Zen there were those who spent over ten long years to pass one single kōan (for instance Tsuchiya Daian or Matsui Ryōzen); how many years of painful struggle those like Kidō took to pass through the 'one word' kōans of Kamakura Zen! These days people seem to expect to pass through dozens of kōans in a year, and it cannot be called the same thing at all. Perhaps it might seem pointless to bring out this text now. After the passing of Master Shinjō, there are no more teachers who use Kamakura Zen kōans in their interviews, and again laymen who have actually come under the hammer of this Zen now number only nine, all of them in their seventies or eighties. It is to prevent it falling into untimely oblivion that I bring out this work, so that the fragments which Shunpō Rōshi left shall not be entirely wasted.

The old manuscripts stocked since 1919 in the Dōkai-in repository of Kenchōji were taken out and aired on 1 September 1924, and in the great earthquake more than half of them were destroyed. The records of warrior Zen in particular, held under the collapsed building, became drenched with rainwater and entirely ruined. Thus it has become impossible to make a critical collation of the records, but fortunately from the hundreds of extracts already made, and annotated over many years, it has been possible to investigate Kamakura Zen and to bring out this collection of a hundred kōans properly edited. Some of the detail had to be determined by comparing as well as possible with what remained of the documents ruined by the earthquake, referring back also to the very many notes which I had myself taken earlier.

Since the earthquake, I have lived the Zen life, for a time in a retreat in Kyūshū, and now buried in my books at Sōfukuji temple. What remained from the earthquake has had to be left. But with my old sick body, it has been impossible to complete the full study of Kamakura Zen quickly, so first of all the full text of just the Shōnankattōroku is to be brought out.

In the autumn of 1919 I received from Mr Nakayama Takahisa (Ikkan) all the notes about warrior Zen left by the late Shunpō, rōshi of Daitokuji, and to help me with these I examined the old records in the repositories of the Kamakura temples. At that time thanks to the kindness of the kanchō of Kenchōji, the old records of the Donge room were moved to the study in my lodgings there, so that I was able to examine the records of Zen of old masters of many different periods. Again I must express gratitude for the co-operation of Zen master Kananawa, head of the sect administration, thanks to which my examination of documents and records from their stock of rare manuscripts was made so fruitful. Also I was permitted by the priests in charge to go over the records preserved in the repositories of Jufuku, Butsunichi, Garyū and Hōju temples, which provided some precious material on old Zen.

Now by good fortune the manuscript of Shōnankattōroku is ready for publication, and I wish to set down my deepest gratitude and appreciation in regard to all those who have helped so much in the task.

Imai Fukuzan Spring 1925

EXTRACTS FROM IMAI FUKUZAN'S INTRODUCTION TO WARRIOR ZEN

According to the Nyūdōsanzenki (Records of Lay Zen) – the postscript of the first volume of the manuscript of Zenkō and the introduction to volume eight of the Kenchō manuscripts – the Zen training of warriors at Kamakura fell into two stages. Up to the end of the Muromachi period (1573), incidents from the training of the early warrior disciples were set as kōans to beginners, and only afterwards were the classical kōans concerning Buddhas and patriarchs used extensively. The incidents from the Zen training of warriors were the kind recorded in the Shōnankattōroku.

But after the end of the Muromachi era, it became common among teachers to present warriors with nothing but classical kōans from the very beginning, and those who used the incidents from warrior training as kōans gradually became very few. So that the three hundred odd kōans of warrior Zen which are known to have existed in Kamakura Zen came to be forgotten.

Among the teachers after Hakuin (died 1768 at age of eighty-four) there were still some who presented these incidents to pupils, but they were not set as kōans to be wrestled with and answered in interviews with the teacher. There were some who, when a pupil stuck too long over one of the classical kōans, brought out one of these old stories of the early samurai as a means to get him round the obstacle and bring him on to the right path from a new direction. In the interviews given by teachers of the Hakuin line, it can be said that no more than twelve or thirteen of the incidents from the training of warriors were known. Only in the Sōryūkutsu (blue dragon cave) line were there still over a score of them in use.

However, teachers of the line from Kogetsu (died in 1751 aged eighty-five; founder of Fukujuji in Kurume, Kyūshū) had a great deal to do with samurai, and in their interviews they preserved a trádition of this Zen, as suited to the inclination of their pupils. They used over a hundred such kōans. The Sōrinzakki (Zen Analects) and Bukedōshinshū (Records of Warriors Aspiring to the Way) list three hundred warrior kōans, but in the Kogestu tradition one who could pass through seventy-two of them was reckoned to have a complete mastery of the whole three hundred. In the interviews only 108 were being actually set as kōans, and to solve the seventy-two main ones was to pass the whole collection. After the Meiji Restoration (1868) the last teachers to use them were Shinjō of the Hakuin line, and Shunnō of the Kogetsu line, and there were none who followed them in this, so that at present (1920) there are no teachers who use them. Thus there are very few today who know anything about the incidents recorded in the Nyūdōsanzenki and the other collections.

By the end of Muromachi the Kamakura kōans were gradually being forgotten, and in the Zen which followed Hakuin they were almost entirely discarded. There was however still some tradition about them in Kyūshū, and at the time of the Meiji Restoration Zen teachers all over the country were continually being asked about this Zen by samurai of the main Kyūshū clans like Satsuma and Chōshū. Many Rinzai teachers found they could not answer. However in the Sōtō line, Ekidō the abbot of Sōjiji temple, Kankei the abbot of Eiheiji, Bokusan of Kasuisai, and others knew warrior Zen well, and could meet the questions of the Kyūshū civilians and warriors.

In the Rinzai line, there was an impression that samurai Zen had been Zen of repeating the Name of Amida (nembutsu Zen), and the teachers did not know about the Kamakura kōans. Gyōkai, abbot of Zōjōji, of the Jōdo sect, and Tetsujō, abbot of Chionin, and other spiritual leaders of this line taught samurai Zen as being Nembutsu, and often preached to the high officials and generals of those times. The teachers of other lines knew the stories, but simply related them and did not set them as kōans to be wrestled with. And in fact what goes on in the interview room is different with each line, and is not something that ought to be lightly spoken about.

Warrior Zen began with the samurai who came to Eisai at Jufukuji in Kamakura, from 1215. (This temple was burnt down in 1247 and again in 1395, many of the records being lost.) Historically this Zen was taught in the interviews of Rinzai masters, but now there are few within the Rinzai lines who know of it, though quite some outside who have some knowledge. This is an ironic fact, on discovering which many inquirers into Zen have had to suppress a smile.

In the first years of Meiji, the Daikyō-in in Tōkyō began work examining old records in Zen temples, collaborating with some priests of the Rinzai line as well. (The Daikyō-in was set up with some official support to advise on religious matters.) A glance at their bulletin makes the facts clear. Temples all over the country sent old records concerning warrior Zen to the Daikyō-in for examination. The material was there classified under five heads: Zen connected with the Imperial palace, with the Shōgun rulers, with nobles, with the gentry of various clans, and with simple warriors. Those parts which recorded kōans were collated. This project was initiated at the suggestion of a monk named Taikōan. It was found that the Rinzai temples, obsessed with the principle 'no setting up of words', had not merely seen little necessity to keep records, but were very indifferent to the preservation of what records did exist. So there is very little material about what kōans the teachers gave to the princes, to the nobles, to the warriors and to the ordinary people. Again, one incident which takes up five or six pages in records of the Sōtō and Ōbaku Zen lines, in the Rinzai account may have barely half a page, so that sometimes it is quite difficult to make out all the main points. There are those who maintain that this is in accordance with the principle of directness, that 'just one inch of the blade kills the man', but if this principle is applied to historical records, along with the other one of not setting up words in the first place, surely it is going too far.

Parts of the Daikyō-in records have been damaged by insects and so on, but what follows is a list of the published collections of records which were then available to them.

The *Hōmeishū* (Record of the cry of the phoenix – in the records of Kenninji) and the *Undaigendan* (Discourses from the cloud dais – records of Nanzenji) in reporting the same incidents differ only in the length and detail of their accounts. Both of them begin with the interviews between the Empress Tachibana (Danrin), consort of Emperor Saga, and the Chinese Zen master Gikū, about AD 815, and follow with an account of the interest taken in Zen by sixteen emperors, from Gotoba (1183–98) up to Go-mizuno-o (1611–29). Both of them have the imperial utterances expressed in classical Yamatokotoba, which are thus difficult to read without a translation into standard language. For this reason Shunpō himself had the impression that these are paraphrases of old Court documents. However a copy in possession of Ekidō of Sōjiji was finally discovered which turned out to have these sections all transcribed into orthodox Chinese characters and thus easy to read.

Sōrinzakki (Zen analects) and a commentary on it were pieced together by Shunpō from various copies of parts of it which existed in the Kyōto temples, though owing to the fragmentary nature of the material he was never able to reconstruct a complete original text. In any case none of the Kyōto copies have anything before Ōnin (1467) and they stop at Genroku (1688), so that they cannot be compared with the detailed historical accounts in the Kamakura records. The most complete version of the Sōrinzakki and its commentary existed in Zenkōji in Kamakura, but even this goes no further than 1716 and can tell us nothing after that.

Bukedōshinshū (Records of warriors aspiring to the Way – no connection at all with the published book of the same name) is a collection of biographies of warriors who entered Zen training, took interviews with a teacher for some years, and were given a Zen name by the teacher when they had mastered the principle of Zen.

Bushōsōdan (Zen stories of warriors and generals) and *Ryueizenna* (Zen tales of willow camp) give accounts of Zen incidents from the lives of generals from Hōjō Tokiyori up to the Tokugawas. In the Jufukuji library these two have been bound together as an appendix to the Bukedōshinshū, with the title Bumontetsuganzei (pupil of the warrior eye). This was written out by priest Gettei of the Jufukuji sub-temple Keikōan.

Nyūdōsanzenki (Accounts of lay Zen) and *Gosannyūdōshū* (Lay training at Rinzai temples) are accounts of warriors training at the five temples of Kamakura.

Shōnankattōroku (Record of Kamakura kōans) has a hundred kōans consisting of incidents from the training of warriors. A full account of this book is given in the other appendix.

Ka-an-zatsuroku (Analects of Ka-an) is a random collection of notes of incidents concerning the warriors, nobles and officials who came from all over the country to priest Ka-an at Manjuji. At the beginning of the Meiji era many temples had manuscript copies of this, but now (1920) there is only one copy, consisting of twelve fascicules copied by Sōkū of Hōkokuji.

Zendōguzūki (Record of the propagation of Zen) begins with the meeting at Jufukuji between Eisai and Gyōyū, and gives further accounts of Zen training in Rinzai temples up to Ō-ei (1394). There is a manuscript copy in the library at Nirayama.

Zenjōmonshōkan (Mirror of Zen samādhi) consists of biographies of warriors who trained under Zen teachers and finally received the full 'approval' (inka) from them. This book extracts from the accounts in Bukedōshinshū, Gosan-nyūdōshū and others those cases where the master finally gave approval to the pupil as having completed the training.

This book was at Kanazawa before the partial dispersal of the library there, and is known to bibliophiles as an 'ex-Kanazawa book', as in the case also of Shōinmanpitsu (Jottings from the shade of the banana tree), Zenrinrōeishū (Zen songs of retainers), Shōchōshū (Pine and sea), Towa-fūsōshū (Wind and seaweed of eastern Japan), Sekirozakki (Jottings from a stone hearth), Shōtōseigo (Holy words from pine and tide), Fukugenrenpeki (Wall round the front of bliss), Hamanomezarashi (Vision of the beach), Kaenshū (Flowering hedge anthology), and others. All these record incidents of the warrior Zen tradition, and also some of them give poems which the warriors composed as answers to the kōan tests. (This kind of answer is technically called agyo.)

In 1400 Zen master Daigaku Shūei made an examination of the Kanazawa library and catalogued the Zen manuscripts. Later Zenju, the 178th Master of Kenchōji, when he became the teacher at Ashikaga college, examined the old manuscripts at the Kanazawa and Nirayama libraries, and catalogued many hundreds of the old Zen records which he found there. The Zen teachers who were members of Daikyō-in, in their search for accounts of warrior Zen, found and borrowed for examination, through the librarian Suzuki Sōei, many of the old manuscripts there. The examination made it clear that the kōans about which officials and warriors at the beginning of the Meiji era were asking Rinzai teachers, were in fact very early incidents of the training of warriors by teachers of this same Rinzai sect.

No one can estimate how many hundreds and thousands of lay people have practised Zen in Japan since the Empress

Danrin at the beginning of the ninth century, and there must have been innumerable records of the kōans set to them. The first time I saw any material on warrior Zen was in 1872 or 73, when Zen master Bokusan presented my father with a notebook made by the Sōtō master Gattan, and a manuscript written by Zuiun of the Ōbaku sect. From these I got some idea of how teachers of Sōtō and Ōbaku used to handle their warrior pupils in the past. Then after attending the addresses in Tōkyō given by Shunpō, rōshi of Daitokuji, about the old records like Bushōsōdan and Bukedōshinshū, I discovered the still more drastic means which were used in the Rinzai sect for warriors. Later, Bairyō, kanchō of Nanzenji, gave me copies of Undaigendan, Hōmeishū and other texts, from which I came to know about the direct Zen traditions which there had been at the Imperial palace. Only after seeing the Shōnan-kattōroku text which Yamaoka Tesshū had received from Shōjō of Ryūtaku temple in Izu, did I first come to know that there had been a separate Zen tradition at Kamakura.

In 1872, Master Tekisui was elected general head to represent the three Zen sects, and there were many laymen training in Zen. Master Shunpō too was active in the Daikyō-in, and many leading figures in Zen were studying warrior Zen traditions; material about it was being collected in Tōkyō so that there were good opportunities to study the kōans of that tradition. But as in the case of the Hōmeishū text, where the Imperial utterances in the palace tradition were reported in Yamatokotoba, here too there was much use of classical Japanese words of antiquity, which could not be understood without a gloss in contemporary Japanese. In the Kamakura records again, there are many local words from several centuries previously. To read the records themselves one has to peruse an old manuscript entitled 'Old Deer-brush' by Master Sanpaku (156th Master of Enkakuji), and then one has to know the obsolete words. Furthermore, the founders of all the Kamakura temples were Chinese of the Sung or Yüan dynasties, and in the old accounts there is much Chinese transcribed phonetically in a distorted way by writers who did not understand it. Without the glossary compiled by Ryūha, the 178th Master of Kenchōji, there are many passages which could hardly be read, let alone understood. In an old Zenkōji record (which was still preserved in Jufukuji around 1868) there is a report of a meeting between Hōjō Tokimune and Bukkō Kokushi, and in it comes this: 'Kun-sun-rii, kun-sun-rii, raunau, ya-shi-yan-kin-gu-a'. Today there is hardly a soul who could read this and understand it. It was always supposed that it must have been some kōan. Round about 1873, when there were many great figures in Zen coming and going round the Daikyō-in, there was no one, not even Shunpō Rōshi who was consultant professor to the three head temples Daitokuji, Myōshinji and Kenninji, who could suggest any meaning for this Sung Chinese which Bukkō spoke to Tokimune. Nobody had any idea what it was. But when the glossary by Ryūha was acquired by the Daikyō-in, the passage kun-sun-rii ... turned out surprisingly to be 'Come in, come in! I have something to say to Your Honour.' This caused general laughter. In the Kamakura temples there are many similar old records of Sung Chinese transcribed phonetically. So there are many inconveniences in the study of warrior Zen there. But after being presented with the Reikenroku (Record of the spiritual sword – the copy in the Butsunichi-an is called Jintōroku) with the red-ink notes by Kaigan Rōshi and textual amendments by Tōkoku Rōshi, I found that the bulk of the 300 warrior kōans recorded in the Sōrinzakki and elsewhere were Kamakura Zen.

For his research on old Kamakura Zen, Shunpō made many notes on the backs of used pieces of paper. (He almost never used a clean sheet, but always the backs of pieces of wrapping paper and so on. The only time he used a new sheet of paper was for a final fair copy.) Before he could collate all his material into a text, he had to return to Kyōto in 1875, on account of urgent affairs connected with the administration of the colleges attached to the great temples there – so I heard indirectly from others. No one else who had been studying warrior Zen had completed any of the drafts either, and finally it was left to the general research council of ten Zen temples (I recall that this was founded in 1875), which entrusted it to Imagita Kōsen Rōshi. At that time however he was himself engaged in many projects, and from Enkakuji was promoting Zen vigorously in the Kantō area. He became head of the seven lines of the Rinzai sect, and with all his administrative engagements had no time for examining ancient records. He therefore divided the task among the many laymen who were training under him.

Ichinyo (Miyata Chūyū), Ryūmon (Hirata Yasumaru) and others examined the records of Zen at the palace; Mumon (Ōi Kiyomichi), Rakuzan (Suzuki Yoshitaka) and others took the documents on shōgun Zen; Ryōzen (Ishii Tokihisa), Katei (Yamada Toshiaki) and others studied warrior Zen; Daian and Kidō worked solely on Kamakura Zen. But many of them had official duties and little time for the research, and if they were sent abroad it had to be set aside. Moreover those officials in the ministries of Education and the Army who had given support round about 1878, were completely occupied with their political responsibilities when the Satsuma rebellion broke out, and had no opportunity for anything else. Senior men like Ōtori Keisuke and Soejima had to carry out diplomatic missions abroad, and the interest in warrior Zen slipped into the background.

After the death of Yamaoka Tesshū in 1889, those who could say anything on this kind of Zen gradually became few; Katsu Kaishū, Takahashi Deishū, Shimao Tokuan and other great Zen laymen died, and almost no one knew anything about the subject. While the Daikyō-in existed in Tōkyō there were a good many among the Zen teachers who knew about this laymen's Zen, and there were many who used Zen stories of the warriors. As we can see from their recorded sermons, Masters Dokuon and Keichū were speaking on palace Zen,

Mugaku, Teizan and Shunpō on warrior Zen in general, and Kōsen and Shinjō on Kamakura Zen in particular. But as there was nobody who could present Kamakura Zen apart from the dozen kōans which were given in interviews, teachers who had not seen texts like the Sōrinzakki and its commentary tended to think that Kamakura Zen was nothing more than these dozen kōans – perhaps to the quiet amusement of men like Tesshū and Kaishū. But Shunpō Rōshi on the other hand had heard the discourses of Master Myōhō of Hōfukuji (at Iyama in Bicchū) on the Bukedōshinshū, Reikenroku, Bushōsōdan and so on, and knew well about the Kamakura kōans, information which he transmitted to inquirers in Tōkyō; those who wanted warrior Zen called him prince of teachers.

In 1875 he left Tōkyō and in March two years later passed away in Kyōto. It is just fifty years since his death, and there are left in Tōkyō only nine people who came into touch with his greatness, all of them fine vigorous old men. Talking to them about the teacher and about Kamakura Zen, one has the strong feeling of how Zen has changed. For the fiftieth anniversary in March this year, Zen master Nyoishitsu of Sōfukuji desires to distribute some work of Shunpō as a 'fan for the eternal breeze of the Way'. But the only draft which the teacher left was one called Shōkaigifu (Voyager on the ocean of the absolute), which was not concerned with warrior Zen, and all the rest was no more than notes not yet written up into a text.

When I looked through these notes and fragments formerly, I noticed that a great number were concerned with Kamakura Zen; but to arrange these miscellaneous scraps written on the backs of used pieces of paper into a connected text was not something that could be done in a hurry. It would have been impossible, with the limitations imposed by the publication plan, to write up everything connected with Kamakura Zen. So it came about that Master Nyoishitsu began to press for the publication, on the fiftieth anniversary, of a first part only.

No. 1 The Grave of Shunpō

This was to be an edited and supplemented edition of the Shōnankattōroku.

The whole work projected is to be called Bushizenkienshū (Records of warrior Zen training) and the present text is to be just a first part. I have been told that there are in existence 3,600 pages about warrior Zen, bound into thirty-six volumes of a hundred pages each, which have been produced by laymen under the direction of great Zen teachers. And I have wondered whether it might be possible to put them into permanent form. With the loss of so many of the old manuscripts in the Kantō earthquake, it is not feasible to collect and collate all the material in a short time. All I can hope is, that one day I shall complete the work on warrior Zen, of which this Shōnankattōroku is to be the first part. I am a retired scholar already over seventy, and writing is more and more a burden. But I have a dharma-link with my old teacher Shunpō, whose discourses I so often attended, and I rejoice that the draft of the work has been completed for publication of the fiftieth anniversary of his passing. I beg the indulgence of readers for faults they may find in it.

Imai Fukuzan 1925

KAMAKURA KŌANS

No. 1. *The mirror of Enkakuji*

Regent Tokiyori founded the great temple of Kenchōji for the teaching of Buddhism, but the temple soon could not accommodate all the many warriors who became students (nyūdō) in order to enter the Buddhist path and give all their free time to it. So in the first year of Kōan (1278) Tokimune, Tokiyori's son, decided to build another great temple, and invited priest Rankei (afterwards Daikaku) to choose the Brahma-ground, as the site for a temple is called. Teacher and regent walked together round the nearby hills, and found the ruins of a Shingon temple (of the mantra sect) where Minamoto Yoshiyori had once set up a pagoda of Perfect Realization. They decided on this as the place to plant the banner of the Law.

First the teacher performed a purification, and made three strokes with a mattock; then the regent made three strokes, and planted a stalk of grass to mark the spirit of faith.

In the winter of the same year, when Tokimune was having the area prepared for the foundations, a buried stone coffer was found. In it was a perfect circular mirror; engraved on the back were the words EN KAKU – Perfect Realization. So the temple was called Enkakuji.

Taira Masatsuna, a nyūdō student of Zen, at an interview with Mugaku (later Bukkō), told him this story of how the temple came to be called Enkakuji. The teacher said:

'Leave for a moment that perfect mirror buried underground:

No. 2 Regent Hōjō Tokiyori

the perfect mirror at this instant in your hands, what is it? Try and bring it out of its stone coffer. If you don't get this, the spiritual pagoda of Perfect Realization will not be built.'

TESTS

(1) When the stone coffer is broken open, what is that perfect mirror like? *(Imai's note: It is said that this question means, When man dies, what happens to his spirit?)*
(2) Beneath the feet of the man of the Way, as he walks, is the Brahma-ground for the temple. At this instant, try building the pagoda of Perfect Realization.

This incident became a kōan in Kamakura Zen at the interviews of Butsuju, the 21st teacher at Enkakuji.

No. 2. *Hachiman asks to hear the dharma*

When Daikaku was living at Kenchōji temple, the old pines by the lake – which is in the form of a heart – began to bend of themselves. The monks wondered, and asked the teacher about it. The teacher said:

'The god Hachiman comes; he treads on the pines as he comes to ask me about the dharma. And so the pines are bowed.'

(Imai's note: This has to be understood in a Zen sense.)

TESTS

(1) What did Daikaku really mean by saying that the god trod on the pines and so they became bowed?
(2) Right now the god Hachiman is treading on this old back as he comes to ask about the dharma, and so my back is bowed. O monks of the congregation, do you know how to hear the dharma in your spiritual experience?

This incident became a kōan in Kamakura Zen from the time of the interviews of Nanzan, the 20th teacher at Kenchōji.

No. 3.   *Saving Kajiwara's soul*

On the fifteenth day of the seventh month of the sixth year of Kenchō (1255), the rite of Feeding the Hungry Ghosts was being performed at the Karataka mountain gate of Kenchōji temple. When the sūtra reading had been completed, however, priest Rankei (Master Daikaku) suddenly pointed to the main gate and shouted:

'A knight has come through the gate. It is Kajiwara Kagetoki, of many treacheries. Bring him to salvation quickly!'

The monks all stared hard at the gate, but could see no knight there. Only the head monk shouted, 'Clear to see!' He left the line and went back to the Zen hall.

Then the teacher berated the others, saying:

'Look at the crowds of you, supposed to be saving myriad spirits in the three worlds, and yet you cannot save one knight – blind clods! The rite must be performed again at the main gate, and the Heart Sūtra recited in its original Sanskrit.'

So the whole ceremony was transferred from the mountain gate to the main gate, and the Sūtra was recited there in Sanskrit.

After the recitation was over, the monks hurried to the Zen hall and asked the head monk, 'How did *you* see the knight?'

He replied: 'With the eye of the crown of the head, bright and clear!'

TESTS

(1) Put aside for the moment the question of Kajiwara Kagetoki's apparition at Kenchōji, do you see the knight coming galloping his horse across the garden to the interview room here? If you can, save him quickly!

(2) What was the virtue of chanting the sūtra in Sanskrit at the main gate? Say!

(Imai's note: The point of this second test is, Can chanting the Heart Sūtra in Sanskrit bring salvation to Kajiwara, or can it not? He who says it can, shows that he will have to come under the teacher's hammer yet again. Until one has passed this kōan, his reading of the sūtras, whether as monk or layman, is equally meaningless. The kōan must not be taken lightly.)

This first became a kōan in Kamakura Zen at the interviews of Daisetsu, the 47th master of Kenchōji.

No. 4   Daikaku's one-word sūtra

At the beginning of the Kenchō era (1249), 'Old Buddha' Daikaku was invited from Kyōto by the shōgun Tokiyori to spread Zen in the East of Japan. Some priests and laymen of other sects were not at all pleased at this, and out of jealousy spread it around that the teacher was a spy sent to Japan by the Mongols; gradually more and more people began to believe it. At the time the Mongols were in fact sending emissaries to Japan, and the shōgun's government, misled by the campaign of rumours, transferred the teacher to Kōshū. He was not the least disturbed, but gladly followed the karma which led him away.

Some officials there who were firm believers in repetition of the formula of the Lotus, or in recitation of the name of Amida, one day came to him and said: 'The Heart Sūtra which is read in the Zen tradition is long and difficult to read, whereas Nichiren teaches the formula of the Lotus which has only seven syllables, and Ippen teaches repetition of the name of Amida, which is only six. The Zen Sūtra is much longer, and it is difficult to get through it.'

The teacher listened to all this and said: 'What would a

No. 3 Zen master Daikaku (Rankei) (1213–79) painted in 1271, when he was fifty-eight, and had been in Japan twenty-five years

follower of Zen want with a long text? If you want to recite the Zen sūtra, do it with *one word*. It is the six- and seven-word ones which are too long.'

TEST

Master Setsuō used to present his pupils with this story as the riddle of Daikaku's One-word Sūtra. He would say to them: 'The golden-faced teacher (Buddha), it is said, in all his forty-nine years of preaching never uttered a single word. But our Old Buddha (Daikaku) declares one word to lead the people to salvation. What is that word, say! What is that one word? If you cannot find it your whole life will be spent entangled in creepers in a dark cave. If you can say it, with that leap of realization you will pervade heaven and earth.'

(Imai's note: Those who were set this riddle over the years tried the word 'heart', and the word 'Buddha', or 'dharma', 'God', 'mantra', but none of them hit it. When the pearly sweat runs down the body, coming and going for the interviews with the teacher, the one word will be met directly.)

This became a kōan in Kamakura Zen at the interviews of Setsuō, the 151st master at Kenchōji.

No. 5. *Bukkō's no-word sūtra*

Ryō-A, a priest of the Tsurugaoka Hachiman shrine, came to Magaku, (National teacher Bukkō, who succeeded Daikaku) and told him the story of Daikaku's one-word sūtra. He said: 'I do not ask about the six or seven syllables recited by other sects, but what is the one word of Zen?'

The teacher said: 'Our school does not set up any word; its dharma is a special transmission outside scriptures, a truth transmitted from heart to heart. If you can penetrate through to that, your whole life will be a dhāranī (Buddhist mantra), and your death will be a dhāranī. What would you be wanting with a word or half a word? The old master Daikaku went deep into the forest and put *one word* down there, and now the whole Zen world is tearing itself to pieces on the thorns, trying to find it. If the reverend Ryō-A before me wishes to grasp that one word, then without opening the mouth, do you recite the sūtra of no-word. If you fail in your awareness of the no-word, you will at once lose the one word. Displayed, the one word is set above the thirty-three heavens; buried, it is at the bottom of the eighth great hell. Yet in all four directions and above and below, where could it ever be hidden? At this instant before Your Reverence! Is there a word, or is there not?'

The golden needle did not penetrate (the embroidered cloth of the priest's mind), and he silently took his leave.

TEST
Say a word for the priest.

This incident became a kōan in Kamakura Zen at the interviews of Gyokkei, the 131st master at Enkakuji.

No. 6.   *Daikaku's one-robe Zen*

A priest from the headquarters of the regent Yasutoki visited Kenchōji and remarked to Daikaku: 'Eisai and Gyōyū began the propagation of Zen here in Kamakura, but the two greatest teachers of the way of the patriarchs have been Dōgen (of the Sōtō sect) and Bennen (later National Teacher Shōichi). Both of them came to Kamakura at the invitation of regent Tokiyori to teach Zen, but both left before a year was out. So there are not many among the warriors here who have much understanding of Zen. In fact some are so ignorant about it that they think the character for Zen – written as they think by combining the characters for 'garment' and 'single' – means just that. They believe that Zen monks of India in the mountains practised special austerities, and even in winter wore only one cotton robe, and that the name of the sect arose from this.'

No. 4 Zen master Daikaku

Zen

'One-Robe'

Daikaku listened to all this and laughed:

'The people of Kamakura are right to say that Zen means wearing a single garment. They well understand what the sect stands for. An ordinary man is clad in layers of the three poisons and five desires, and though by repetition of the Buddha-name and reading the scriptures he tries again and again to strip them off, he cannot get out of his layers of passions. Fundamentally Zen means having no layers of clothes but just one piece. Repeating the Buddha-name – it is becoming just one piece with the Buddha; reading the scriptures – it is "apart from the Law, no I, and without I no Law", so that I and the Law are one piece.'

This is called *bringing everything to one*. The warriors of Kamakura, when they say Zen means the sect of a single robe, have grasped its deepest essence.

'Without those layers of clothes, you should cultivate the field of the elixir (tanden) in the Zen way. Here and now let Your Reverence strip off the 80,000 robes of the dharma treasury of scripture. How is it, the bare purity under the one robe?'

The priest bowed in reverence and left.

TESTS

(1) Try stripping off the layers of clothes which you have been sewing for beginningless age.
(2) After the 80,000 robes of the dharma treasury of scripture have been stripped off, what is the single garment that remains? Speak!

(3) One cannot go naked in the street; show your single robe.
(4) Leave for a moment becoming one piece with the Buddha, and try here and now becoming one with the teacher.

This began to be used as a kōan in Kamakura Zen at the interviews of Kosen, the 38th master at Kenchōji.

Variant on No. 6.   Bukkō's loin-cloth Zen

On the staff of Yasutsura Genbansuke, a minister of Hōjō Yasutoki, was one Morikatsu who was a nyūdō student of Zen. Once when he came to Enkakuji he met one of Bukkō's attendants named Isshin, and said to him:

'That stupid crowd at Kamakura don't know how to write the name of our sect with the proper character, but get it mixed up with the character for "loin-cloth". They're an odd lot.'

Zen

'loin-cloth'

The attendant was distressed that people should thus casually degrade the word Zen, and mentioned the matter to the teacher, who laughed and said:

'Loin-cloth is indeed the great concern of our Zen gate, and those Kamakura soldiers must not be condemned for lack of learning. What gives the life to men is the power of the front gate (of men and women), and when they die, it ends with the (excretion at the) back gate. Is not this life-and-death the great concern of our Zen gate? And what contains the organs of life and death is the loin-cloth. If you penetrate into that which contains both, you will know where life comes from and where death goes to. Now use the loin-cloth to demonstrate our teaching to that little bit of an idiot, and get him to try to find out how it is when the loin-cloth is annihilated.'

Isshin went and brandished a loin-cloth before Morikatsu's face, saying: 'All living beings are wriggling about within the loin-cloth. When you annihilate the loin-cloth, how is it?'

Morikatsu had no words.

TEST
Bring a word for Morikatsu.

This began to be used as a kōan in Kamakura Zen with Kosen, the 38th master at Kenchōji.

No. 7. *The bucket without a bottom*

(Imai's note: The nun Mujaku, whose lay name was Chiyono, was a woman of Akita who married and had one daughter. In 1276 when she was thirty-four her husband died, and she could not get over the grief. She became a nun, and trained under Bukkō. The story is that on the evening of a fifteenth day of August, when she was filling her lacquer flower-bucket where the valley stream comes down, the bottom fell out; seeing the water spilling she had a flash of insight, and made a poem on it to present to the teacher.

Later he set her a classical kōan, Three Pivot-phrases of Ōryū, and examined her minutely on it, and she was able to meet the questions. Again she continued interviews with him for a long time, and in the end he 'passed over the robe and bowl', namely authorized her as a successor to teach. Uesugi, Nikaidō and others had built Keiaiji temple in Kyōto, and asked her to become the first teacher there. It was not unusual in Zen for a teacher to be a woman.

After Bukkō died, a hermitage called Shōmyakuan was built for her at Shirogita to be the temple of Bukkō's grave.

She died in November of 1298 at the age of seventy-six.
(There is some discrepancy in the dates – Tr.))

Mujaku, whose lay name was Chiyono, came to Bukkō, Teacher of the Nation, and said, 'What is Zen?'

The teacher said, 'The heart of the one who asks is Zen; it is not to be got from the words of someone else.'

The nun said: 'Then what is the teacher doing, that he gives sermons and they are recorded?'

(Imai's note: Bukkō's Japanese being inadequate, he gave his sermons in Sung Dynasty Chinese; they were recorded and afterwards translated, to be distributed to his Japanese followers. This is what the nun is referring to.)

The teacher said: 'To a deaf man, you show the moon by pointing; to a blind man, you show the gate by knocking on it with a tile.'

At that moment one of the deer near the Hakugandō stream gave a cry. The teacher said, 'Where is that deer?'

The nun listened. The teacher gave a Katzu! shout and said: 'Who is this listening?'

At these words the nun had a flash of illumination, and went out. At the water-pipe from the Hakugandō she took up a lacquered wooden bucket for flowers. As she was holding it full of water, she saw the moon's reflection in it, and made a poem, which was presented to the teacher:

> The flower bucket took the stream water and held it,
> And the reflection of the moon through pines lodged there
> in purity

Bukkō could not understand the poem in Japanese, so priest Giō translated it into Chinese and showed it to him. Bukkō glanced at it and said: 'Nun, take the Heart Sūtra and go.'

After that, she had interviews with the master, coming and being sent away, till in the end the lacquer bucket broke, and she presented another poem, of this realization:

The bottom fell out of Chiyono's bucket;
Now it holds no water, nor does the moon lodge there.

(Imai's note: In the account in Zenmonkaikiden the version is: Chance or design? The bottom fell out of her bucket; Now it holds no water, nor does the moon lodge there.)

After Chiyono's death, the nun Nyozen of Tōkeiji used to meditate on this poem as her basic theme. Nyozen's lay name was Takihime *(or Takino according to the account in the Bukedōshinshū – Imai)*, and she had been of the household of Ōi Toshiharu, a retainer of the Uesugi family. She trained under Genō, the founder of Kaizōji temple, and in 1313 she grasped the essence of Zen, presenting this poem to her teacher:

The bottom fell out of the bucket of that woman of humble
   birth;
The pale moon of dawn is caught in the rain-puddles

TESTS

(1) What does the poem about the water from the water-pipe caught in the bucket really mean?
(2) What really is the bucket without a bottom?
(3) What is the real meaning of the poem of the nun Nyozen?

These poems were used as kōans at Enkakuji temple itself after the time of Daikō, the 5th teacher, at the beginning of the Shōan era (1299).
(Imai's note: From the Bunroku era (1592), what was called Heart-sūtra Zen became fashionable in Kamakura: a chakugo comment had to be found to fit certain phrases of the Sūtra. The poems of the two nuns came to be used as comments, so a further test came into existence:

(4) What are the phrases from the Heart Sūtra to fit the poems of the nuns? Say!)

No. 8. *Jizō stands up*

When Hōjō Sōun attacked Odawara Castle and was occupying Kantō, the eastern part of Japan, the soldiers of the areas round Kamakura forced their way onto the lands of the temples; as their number gradually increased, Kenchōji was in dire straits.

On a winter day in the first year of Tenmon (1532), the teacher Yakkoku, the 169th master at Kenchōji, disregarding his own illness got up and gave an address from the high seat. Glaring at the congregation, of all ranks, he said:

'Men of great virtue, I ask you this – make the seated Jizō image in this hall stand up!'

Out of this occasion came one of the kōans at Kenchōji. The samurai Mamiya Munekatsu, who had a position as a temple official, confined himself in the great hall where the image was – a wooden Jizō seated on the lotus altar – for twenty-one days, vowing to make the Jizō stand up. He was reciting continuously the mantra of Jizō: OM! KA-KA-KA! BISANMAYE SOWAKA! *(This approximates the Sanskrit which glorifies Ksitigarbha as the smiling one; Ka-ka-ka! represents a great laugh – Tr.)* On the last night of the vow he was running round the hall like a madman, shouting 'Holy Jizō, stand up!'

At two o'clock in the morning the monk who was making the rounds struck the regulation single blow on the sounding-board which hangs in front of the hall. Munekatsu suddenly had a realization, and cried:

'Holy Jizō – it's not that he stands up, and it's not that he sits down. He has a life which is neither standing nor sitting.'

TESTS

(1) See how you can get the sitting Jizō to stand up.
(2) See how you can get the standing Jizō to sit down.
(3) What is the life of Jizō apart from standing or sitting? Say!

No. 5 Jizō stands up

This became one of the Kamakura kōans at the interviews of
Ryōkō when he was the 172nd master at Kenchōji.

No. 6 Jizō sits

No. 9. *Jizō coming out of the hall*

When Nitta Yoshisada's soldiers were burning the countryside in 1331, they attacked the Kamakura temples with fire, and Kenchōji was set alight. It is said that the monk in charge of the main hall put the great image of Jizō on his back and

No. 7 The Great Jizō

carried it to safety. The Jizō was sixteen foot in height and breadth, and weighed over 800 pounds. The doors of the Buddha-hall made an opening of only eight foot. How did the monk carry the Jizō out through that opening?

TESTS
(1) Surely all of you are men of mighty strength? Now try and see! Carry on your back an 800-pound Jizō.
(2) How do you carry out a sixteen-foot image through an eight-foot opening? Say!

37

This began to be used as a kōan at the interviews of Master Ichigen, the 115th teacher at Kenchōji.

No. 10.   *The well of youth*

Since the Minamoto shōgun set up his capital at Kamakura, seventeen times there has been a drought so long that the wells ceased to give water. At those times the country folk came to Kenchōji to draw water from the two wells called Golden Bright and Youth, to allay their thirst. The water of the well of Youth was traditionally reputed to have the special virtue of prolonging life, and invigorating the aged.

The warrior pupil Ōta Kunikiyo brought this up at the end of an interview with Master Seisetsu, the 22nd teacher at Kenchōji. The teacher said:

'Leave for a moment the question whether the well of Youth water can prolong life. Length of life is the number of years between a man's birth and his death, but it is not pre-determined. So how will Your Honour know whether in a particular case the life has been made longer, or shortened?'

The nobleman said: 'I was only mentioning a traditional belief. How should I know what causes the length of life?'

The teacher said: 'Even if one extended his life span by drinking from the well of Youth, still he will not escape death in the end. But at Kenchōji there is also a water of Immortality. He who drinks that, never dies. Does Your Honour know of it? The water of Immortality! When it bubbles up and from what source, there is none who knows; whither it flows and where it goes back to, there is none who knows. Since the government was set up here, seventeen times there have been great droughts, but this has not lessened by one drop; since (the first Emperor) Jimmu, forty-six times have there been great rains, but this has not increased by one drop. Nothing in the world can compare with it in purity and coolness. One drop of it heals all the countless ills of men and nature. He who drinks it, will never die. This old priest will give a drop to Your Honour; I ask you just to open your mouth to receive it.'

The soldier said: 'I cannot open my mouth for that drop.'

The teacher said: 'How is it that you cannot open your mouth?'

The soldier said: 'I suppose I have not trained enough under the iron hammer.'

The teacher said: 'Your mouth is in your own body. Why do you wait for training from another? Do you yourself open it.'

The officer bowed and went out. When he got home he had a realization, and made a poem:

The water of immortality I had thought was in the temple well,

When I returned and looked, was flowing in my own well. *(Imai's note: In the Bukedōshinshū version the poem runs: The water of Immortality I had thought was in the temple well, When I returned and looked, was in my own well too.)*

TESTS

(1) What is the difference between the water of Youth and the water of Immortality? Say!

(2) Drink that water. From your own experience how is it, hot or cold?

This became a kōan in Kamakura Zen in the interviews of Butsuju (literally, Buddha-life), the 30th teacher at Kenchōji.

No. 11. *Putting out the fire in Hell Valley*

In the third month of the tenth year of Kōan (1287) Master Bukkaku built the Eshunan sub-temple in the place called Hell Valley. It had been the execution ground when the Minamoto shōgun Yoritomo founded his government, and the people

39

had a deep dread of the place, as haunted by lost spirits of the executed.

After the sub-temple had been built there, the presence of the lost spirits manifested as an appearance of blue flame coming from under the floor of the kitchen. The teacher was therefore asked to hold a memorial service for them.

That evening he bent double and crept under the floor, pissed on the herd of demons who were visible in the flame, and came out. The magic flame was put out, and never appeared again, and the local people called this the Pissing Memorial Service of Eshunan.

TESTS

(1) The blue flame at Eshunan was put out long ago, but right now, under my stove here, a crowd of lost spirits has appeared. What will you do as a memorial service for them, and what will you do to save them? Say!

(2) If as the story says, in the old days they had to use piss and shit for a mere memorial service, what would they use for the rite of salvation? Show the proof!

This incident became a kōan in Kamakura Zen from the interviews of Kosen, the 38th master of Kenchōji.

No. 12. Rankei's shari pearls

On the twenty-fourth day of the seventh month of the first year of Kōan (1276) Master Rankei (Daikaku) passed away, and at the cremation at Kenchōji there were clusters of shari pearls among the ashes. Even the leaves of the trees nearby which had been wreathed in the smoke put forth shari pearls. The ancient tradition says that according to the power of samādhi of the life that has been lived, shari pearls will be many or less, and what happened demonstrated the depth of the samādhi power of Master Rankei.

No. 8 Zen master Daikaku shortly before his death

The Zen pupil Ōta related this to Master Jikusen, the 29th master at Kenchōji, and asked:

'Will there be many shari pearls when you yourself pass away?'

The teacher replied: 'Why wait for death for this old priest's shari pearls? The trees were putting them forth before I was born.'

TESTS

(1) What do shari pearls come from? If you say, from samādhi power, then show some pearls of samādhi power right now.

(2) Leave for a moment the shari pearls after death, but where are the shari pearls before your birth made? Say!

This became a kōan in Kamakura Zen at the interviews of Kaō, the 52nd master at Enkakuji.

No. 13.   *The deer at the sermon*

In the fifth year of Kōan (1282) when Tokimune built the great temple of Enkakuji and National Teacher Bukkō was installed as the founder, the white deer used to assemble in a herd and come to hear the dharma, eyes glistening with tears. At the time there was in Kamakura a hunter who reared fierce hounds which would rush barking through the mountains in pursuit of the prey.

At these times the deer herd was fortunately safe from the teeth of the hounds, assembled as they were in the garden of the sermon hall. It was a blessed omen indeed, and so the temple came to be called the temple of the Blessed Deer; and it is also said that the grass of the place where they grazed came to be called Enkakuji grass.

TESTS

(1) Deer have never been known to understand human speech, so how was it that they wept when they listened to the sermon?

(2) Today you great warriors in the congregation here, all becoming spiritual heroes, have found the great Enkakuji hall right where you stand. Leaving aside the deer for a moment, try giving a sermon to the hounds! Do you demonstrate the proof of what the old teacher was proclaiming.

This incident became a kōan in Kamakura Zen at the interviews of Seisetsu (a Chinese master who died in 1339 in Japan, and whose line became one of the subsects in Japanese Rinzai Zen).

No. 14.   *The snake round the Ginko tree*

In the fourth month of the third year of Kenchō (1249), Priest Rankei (Zen master Daikaku) was at Jōrakuji temple in Kamakura. One of his students, Rōnen, braving the dangers of the night came a long way for an interview, and arrived early in the morning. As he came in the gate, he saw round a ginko tree a white snake, coiled seven and a half times. As Rōnen stared fixedly at it, the scaled form vanished like a dream. When he came to the hall, he told the master's attendant monk about it.

The monk said: 'Benzaiten (the goddess of prosperity) of Enoshima Island reveres the Master, and watches over this temple. What you saw will have been some divine form of hers.'

Rōnen said: 'Can even a long snake get the dharma from the Master?'

The attendant said: 'A long one is a long dharma-body; a short one is a short dharma-body.'

TESTS

(1) Why was the snake-form coiled seven and a half times?
(2) A snake cannot understand human speech; how could it get the dharma from the Master?
(3) What does the attendant's last remark mean?

This incident became a kōan in Kamakura Zen at the interviews of Taikō, the 81st master at Kenchōji.

No. 15.   *The dragon crest*

During a break in the gardening, some of the gardener monks were talking under the pines in the garden behind the abbot's quarters, and it was recalled how in the old days Hōjō Tokimasa (1138–1215; regent 1203–5) as a young man went into retreat at a temple on Enoshima Island, praying for lasting success in his campaigns. On the last night of the twenty-one days' retreat, a beautiful princess in a green robe appeared and prophesied, 'Your line will have the supremacy; the tide of glory is rising to your gate.' She changed into a twenty-foot snake and entered the sea, leaving three fish-like scales on the shore, which Tokimasa took and made into a luminous banner. And so it is said that the great temples of Kenchōji, Enkakuji and others have three fish-scales in their temple crests. Then the monks were arguing about the dragon carved on the pillar of one of the Enkakuji halls, and how it did not have the dragon scales in triangles like the temple crest, and some said that therefore Benzaiten (goddess of prosperity) could not have been a real dragon, and so the talk went round and round.

Master Bukkō overheard this, and came out and said: 'Leave the question of the three scales for a moment, but have any of you in fact seen a dragon?'

The head gardener said: 'No, I have never yet met one to see it.'

The teacher said: 'Then if you have never seen a dragon, how can you argue about how its scales ought to be? You are just like those of other sects who criticize the Buddha-heart sect without ever having had a glimpse of the Buddha heart. If you want to know how the scales ought to be, go to Enoshima for a retreat and pray to the dragon and see one. And you don't need to travel elsewhere or make any long journey. The real Benzaiten is on the crown of everyone's head. Make a meditation retreat here in the Enkakuji meditation hall for twenty-one days. If you are wholly one-pointed you will be able to see a dragon on the last day. If you can't see it on the twenty-first day, practise for twenty-one weeks. And if you still cannot see it, then press on your practice for twenty-one years, all hours of the day and night, never forgetting your resolution, and when the last day comes you will surely meet and see a dragon.'

TESTS

(1) Using the divine powers of the Way, manifest the snake body and the woman form.
(2) How is it when you meet the dragon?
(3) Show the scales before my eyes.

This first became a kōan at the interviews of master Daisetsu, the 40th master of Enkakuji.
(Imai's note: Originally, a monk wishing to enter Enkakuji had to sit in meditation continuously for twenty-one days in accordance with this tradition, but after 1575 it was reduced to seven days.)

No. 16. *The great Buddha of Hase*

Michimasa, a warrior Zen student of Suwa, made a pilgrimage to the Great Buddha of Hase (Kamakura), and on the way back paid a visit to Enkakuji, where he had an interview with priest Daikyū (died 1289). He talked about the circumstances of the construction of the Great Buddha, and showed the paper charm which he had got from the temple there. The teacher asked what was the weight of the Great Buddha.

Michimasa said: 'The Great Buddha has become worn away because these days it is exposed to wind and rain *(after the destruction by storm of the wooden temple in which it was originally housed – Tr.).* So its weight now cannot be what it was when the Buddha was newly made and installed in the hall. Today one cannot know just what its weight would be.'

The teacher said: 'I am not asking about a Great Buddha which can be damaged by wind and rain, but about the Diamond Buddha who is now facing me.

The warrior said: 'Twenty-seven kan *(about 100 kg. – Tr.).'*

'What a featherweight!' exclaimed the teacher. 'How could you manage to carry a charm of the Great Buddha?'

Michimasa said: 'Why, how heavy do I have to be to be able to carry a charm of the Great Buddha?'

The teacher said: 'When you can weigh yourself against the Himalayas.'

TESTS

(1) What is the weight of the Great Buddha?

(2) How is the charm of the Great Buddha made?

(3) Weigh yourself against the Himalayas.

This became a kōan in Kamakura Zen in the interviews of Tentaku, the 41st master of Enkakuji.

No. 17. *Numbering the waves on Yui beach*

Minamoto Munatsune, in the spring of the first year of Shōgen (1259) when he was seventy-five years of age, came to

Kenchōji to become a shaven-headed monk, with the name of Gidō. The great teacher Rankei (namely Daikaku) had a formal interview with him, and taking him to be good spiritual material, set him the riddle of how many waves there are on Yui beach.

Gidō poured out his heart's blood on this for two years, and finally breaking through the confusion he made answer in a Chinese poem:

> In the ocean of the holy dharma
> There is neither movement nor stillness.
> The essence of the wave is like a mirror;
> When something comes, the reflection appears.
> When there is nothing in the mind,
> Wind and waves are both forgotten.

He made a verse in Japanese about his time of practice:

> Two years of wandering on Yui beach.
> There was no need to number off the waves.

TESTS

(1) Count the waves on Yui beach.
(2) What has Gidō's verse about the ocean of the holy dharma got to do with how many waves there are? Say!
(3) What does Gidō's Japanese verse mean?

This incident became a kōan in Kamakura Zen at the interviews given by Ikka, the 145th master at Kenchōji.

(Imai's Note: There are some at the present time who take this kōan of the number of waves at Yui beach as the same thing as the number of hairs on the head which is given in Hakuin's line. But they derive from different traditions. The kōan 'How many hairs are there on your head?' which is used as a test (sassho) comes from a phrase of Gyōzan, whereas the question about the number of waves at Yui, when used in

Kamakura Zen as relating to some words of Ōryū, is naturally not to be understood in the same way. Its ultimate meaning is to be found when the eye is opened under the stick of the master.)

No. 18. *Tokimune's thing below the navel*

(When Tokimune received the news that the Mongol armada was poised to attack Japan, he went in full armour to see Bukkō his teacher, and said: 'The great thing has come,' to which the teacher replied: 'Can you somehow avoid it?' Tokimune calmly stamped his feet, shook his whole body and gave a tremendous shout of Katzu! The teacher said: 'A real lion cub, a real lion roar. Dash straight forward and don't look round!' After the defeat of the Mongols, Tokimune built the great monastery of Enkakuji, and installed in it the representation of Jizō-of-a-thousand-forms. Bukkō became the first teacher there. Tokimune organized a great religious service for the souls of the dead of both sides. Soon afterwards he died at the age of thirty-three. In the funeral oration Bukkō said that he had been a Bodhisattva – 'for nearly twenty years he ruled without showing joy or anger; when the victory came he showed no elation; he sought for the truth of Zen and found it.' – Tr.)

At the outbreak of war in the first year of Kōan (1278) Tokimune visited Bukkō and gave the Katzu! shout of dashing straight forward. Priest Giō said: 'The general has got something great below his navel, so the shout too is great.'

The Field of the Elixir (tanden, the energy-centre an inch below the navel) of Taoist doctrine was called in the Szechuan dialect Shii-ku-ii-mo, the thing under the navel. Giō was a priest from Szechuan who had come with Daikaku to Kenchōji in Japan, and in praising the greatness of Hōjō Tokimune's tanden energy, he used this Szechuan phrase. *(Like many remarks of the Chinese priests, it was transcribed*

No. 9 Jizō of a thousand forms

into Chinese characters, and the Japanese, not knowing the colloquial Szechuan phrase, took it in a literal sense – Tr.)

One of the regent's ministers, Masanori, when he came to know what Giō had said, asked him indignantly:

'When did Your Reverence see the size of what our lord has below his navel?'

The priest said: 'Before the general was born, I saw it.'

The courtier did not understand.

The priest said: 'If you do not understand the greatness of what is below the general's navel, then see through to before you yourself were born, the greatness of the thing below the navel. How would that thing become greater or less by the honour or contempt of high or low?'

The courtier was still more bewildered.

The priest gave a Katzu! shout and said: 'Such is the voice of it, of that thing.'

At these words the courtier had an insight and said: 'This

petty official today has been fortunate enough to receive a Katzu! from you. I have known the greatness of that thing below our lord's navel.'

The priest said: 'What is its length and breadth, say!'

The courtier said: 'Its length pierces the three worlds: its breadth pervades all ten directions.'

The priest said: 'Let the noble officer present a Katzu! of that greatness to show the proof.'

The courtier was not able to open his mouth.

TESTS

(1) What is the meaning of dashing straight ahead?

(2) Say directly, what is the general's dashing straight forward.

(3) Leaving the general's dashing straight forward, what is your dashing straight forward, here and now? Speak!

(4) Leaving your dashing straight forward, what is the dashing straight forward of all the Buddhas and beings of the three worlds?

(5) Leaving the dashing straight forward of the Buddhas and beings, what is the dashing straight forward of heaven and earth and the ten thousand phenomena?

(6) Leaving for the moment the thing below the navel of the Taoists, what is the thing below the navel in our tradition? Say!

(7) Say something about the thing below the navel before father and mother were born.

(8) When the light of life has failed, then say something of that thing below the navel.

(9) Leaving the general's Katzu! – when you yourself are threatened by an enemy from somewhere, what great deed will you perform? Say!

(10) Give a Katzu! for the courtier to prove it.

This became a kōan when Tōrin, 44th master of Kenchōji, began to use it in interviews.

(Imai's note: According to the records in Gosan-nyūdōshū in Kamakura the samurai there were set this kōan and wrestled with it, and even after 'seeing the nature' they were never passed through it for at least five or six years. It is said that 'dash straight forward' in the first tests was often taken in the meaning of 'swiftly' or else 'sincerely' and that these were never passed.)

No. 19. The gate by which all the Buddhas come into the world

Originally Enkakuji was a place forbidden to women, with the exception that unmarried women of a samurai family who were training at Zen were allowed to come and go through the gate. After 1334 a rule was made that unless a woman had attained to 'seeing the nature' she was not allowed to go to the Great Light Hall. In time it became the custom that the keeper of the gate, when a woman applied to go through, would present a test question. According to one tradition from that time *(recorded in the commentary to Sōrinzakki – Imai)*, five tests were in use at the gate of Enkakuji:

TESTS

(1) The gate has many thresholds: even Buddhas and patriarchs cannot get through.
   If you would enter, give the pass-word.
(2) The strong iron door is hardly to be opened.
   Let one of mighty power tear it off its hinges.
(3) Vast outstretched in all directions – no door, no gate.
   How will you recognize the gate?
(4) 84,000 gates open at the same time.
   He who has the eye, let him see.
(5) What is it? this gate by which
   All the Buddhas come into the world.

No. 10 The gate of Enkakuji
      (International Society for Educational Information, Tokyo)

A pupil of Ninpō, the nun teacher at Tōkeiji, was Yoshihime (daughter of General Kanazawa Sada), who was ugly and also exceptionally strong. Her nickname was 'devil-girl'. She wished to have Zen interviews with Old Buddha Seisetsu, and went across to Enkakuji up to the gate. But the gate-keeper monk barred her way with a shout:

'What is it, the gate through which the Buddhas come into the world?'

Yoshihime got hold of his head and forced it between her legs, saying: 'Look, look!'

The monk said: 'In the middle, there is a fragrance of wind and dew.'

Yoshihime said: 'This monk! He's not fit to keep the gate; he ought to be looking after the garden.'

The gate-keeper ran into the temple and reported this to the Master's attendant, who said, 'Let us go down and test this, and see if we can give a twist in there.'

At the gate, he tested her with the question: 'What is it, the gate through which the Buddhas come into the world?'

Yoshihime again got hold of the head and held it between her legs, saying: 'Look, look!'

The attendant said: 'The Buddhas of the three worlds come giving light.'

Yoshihime said: 'This monk is one with the eye; he saw the 84,000 gates thrown open all together.'

TESTS

(1) Say a pass-word for Yoshihime to enter the gate.
(2) Sweep aside the iron door that bars you.
(3) Vast outstretched in all directions: how is that state?
(4) How do you see the 84,000 gates? Say!
(5) What is it, the gate through which the Buddhas come into the world?
(6) What is this 'fragrance of wind and dew'?
(7) I do not ask you about the Buddhas of the three worlds giving light, but how do *you* give light right now?

(Imai's note: Those who do not know Kamakura Zen may give a derisive smile at the gate-keeper's reply: 'In the middle there is a fragrance of wind and dew', and for them I add a few words. The two legs represent the opposites of being and non-being, form and emptiness, ultimate and provisional truth, and so on. The fragrance of wind and dew is the experience of

the Middle Way apart from these opposites. Nevertheless the gate-keeper's response was a very pedestrian one from the Zen point of view, and Yoshihime did not assent to it.)

These tests were given at the interviews of the old master Gyokkei, the 131st teacher at Enkakuji.

No. 20. *The rite of the Treasury of Space*

The officer Nagayasu, who had a position at Jufukuji temple, remarked to Bukkō's attendant Eibin: 'When the founder, National Teacher Bukkō, came to Kamakura and began to teach at Jufukuji, he was so ridiculously short that many of the warriors despised him. At that time they greatly respected men of commanding physique, and had a corresponding contempt for a poor one. They say that the teacher regretted this, and undertook to perform the Esoteric rite called Treasury of Space, for one hundred days. When he first came into the hall to begin, his height was marked by a notch on the pillar in front of the hall, and when the period of a hundred days was up, his height was again measured. He was four inches taller.

'Now in your case too, I can see that as you are very short, some of the warriors are bound to despise you. If you would consent to perform the rite of the Treasury of Space in the same way, and so increase your height, you would receive more reverence and faith from others.'

The attendant Bin said: 'If I perform the rite of the Treasury of Space, how should my stature increase by only four inches? It would more than fill heaven and earth and the four directions.'

Nagayasu said: 'How can that be?'

The attendant said: 'In me there is no long or short. When long and great, heaven and earth put into it still do not fill it:

when short and small, the tip of a hair can contain it. This is what is called the Treasury of Space.'

TESTS

(1) How does the body become taller by performing the rite of the Treasury of Space?

(2) What did Bin mean when he spoke of great and small?

(3) The teacher Nanzan used to present this kōan by saying: 'Here and now, do you perform the rite of the Treasury of Space and increase your stature, to show the sixteen-foot form to me. Let me see it clearly!'

(Imai's note: The sixteen-foot form does not refer to a physical height but means the body of the Buddha. In the Lotus sūtra it says that the bodhisattva Kanzeon manifests the Buddha form. To those who are ready for enlightenment, at once he manifests the Buddha form to teach the dharma. So the meaning of the test is, to show some skilful means in this sense. This is how Imagita Kōsen explained it.)

The incident became a kōan at Kamakura in the interviews of Nanzan (Shiun, 1233–1335), the 11th master at Enkakuji.

No. 21. How priest Isshin saved the ghost

In the summer of the third year of Enkei (1310), the ghost of Hōjō Munekata appeared and cursed the regent Morotoki (his descendant, under whom the Hōjō regime was crumbling). Morotoki was aghast at the apparition, and had the goma rite performed at the Hachiman Shrine and by high priests in the Esoteric sect, but without finding any relief for his fears. On the ninth day of the eleventh month of the same year, he was sitting alone in an arbour, when looking up at the garden before him, he saw the angry ghost of Munekata. He felt a sword thrust through him, vomited blood and fell senseless.

The Confucian scholar Yasumarō being consulted told

him: 'There were such cases in the T'ang Dynasty in China. King Hsuan of Chou, again, had his minister Tu Po executed; afterwards the ghost appeared and the king felt as if an arrow had been shot into his breast. The king died. Then Yao Chang of the Later Shin Dynasty, who had attacked Fu Chien of the Early Shin and taken over his territory, was threatened by the vengeful spirit of Fu Chien which appeared before him in broad daylight. Yao Chang felt himself being run through; he vomited blood and died.

'In view of such cases, this appearance of the departed spirit should not be lightly regarded.'

The nobleman was still more frightened, and ordered auspicious ceremonies to be conducted in Shinto shrines and Buddhist temples, combined with prayers for Morotoki himself, but without avail. He soon died.

The government was reluctant to reveal the circumstances of the death, and simply announced that he had died suddenly. But remarkably, at dusk on the day of death, the regent was seen coming in at the Great Gate of Enkakuji. The priest in charge of the gate, seeing the splendidly attired figure approaching, felt surprised and ran to report to his superior priest Kikō. At this time no one in the temples knew of the death of the regent, and no one therefore had any reason to be suspicious.

But priest Isshin, going to the gate to welcome regent Morotoki with due ceremony, understood that this was a ghost, and cried in his Szechuan Chinese: 'Ō ku nii ra' (hau ko ju lai – Welcome, please enter). At these words the ghost disappeared, and was never heard of again.

TESTS

(1) The ghost of regent Morotoki is right here before you now. Try saving him: show the proof of it.

(2) The phrase Ō-ku-nii-ra is used when inviting someone to come to a place. Where was the invitation to? Say!

This kōan, according to Sōringakki, was given at the interviews of Tentaku, the 31st master of Enkakuji.

No. 22. *Stopping the fighting across the river*

In the first year of Tê Yu (1275) priest Mugaku (Bukkō) had planted the banner of the dharma at Chênju temple in the province of T'ai Chou when the Mongols invaded China and overran the province. The teacher accordingly withdrew to Nêngjên temple in Wên Chou, but next year they came plundering into that province too. When one party of Mongol soldiers attacked Nêngjên temple, everyone fled except the teacher, who sat quietly in the main hall.

(The official) Ch'ên Kuo-hsiang often visited the master as a pupil. The teacher, pointing to the Mongol camp across the Wen river, said,

'There is a rope across the river into the camp. Do you make trial of it.' *(Do you stop the fighting – Imai.)*

Hsiang said: 'How can I make trial of it?'

The teacher suddenly grabbed hold of Hsiang and slapped his face. Hsiang instantly had a realization, and made a bow.

TEST
How can a slap be instant realization?

This was first used as a kōan subject in the interviews of Sei Secchō.

No. 23. *The verse facing death*

In the eighth month of the second year of Tê Yu priest Mugaku (Zen mater Bukkō) when facing death by the sword of a Mongol soldier spoke the verse:

In heaven and earth, no crack to hide;
Joy to know the man is void and the things too are void.
Splendid the great Mongolian long sword,
Its lightning flash cuts the spring breeze

TESTS
(1) Which line contains the essence of all four lines?
(2) Men and things are right before us now; how can one make them out to be void?
(3) What does the phrase about the lightning flash mean?

This kōan began to be used in the interviews of Sei Secchō, the 16th master at Enkakuji.

No. 24. *The Cave of Man in Mount Fuji*

(Imai's note: In the Record of Nine Generations of the Hōjō Rulers, the first part, the following story occurs:

On the third day of the sixth month of the third year of Kennin (1203 A.D.) the Shōgun Yoriie went hunting on the foot-slopes of Mount Fuji, in the country of Suruga. There is a big cave on the lower slope of the mountain which the local people call the Cave of Man. He thought he would like to find out where it led, and called Nitta Shirō Tadatsune; giving him a most precious sword, he told him to go into the cave and explore it to the end. Tadatsune bowed, received the sword and withdrew. At the head of a party of six, he went into the cave. The next day, the fourth, at the hour of the snake (10 a.m.) Shirō Tadatsune came back out of the cave, his journey altogether having taken a day and a night. He was brought before the Shōgun to report, and this was his account.

The cave became very narrow so that it was difficult even to turn round; they had to squeeze through one after another, and as in a nightmare they felt they could hardly move. The darkness was indescribable. The party had each a pine torch;

they kept in touch by calling to each other. A stream running along the bottom soaked their feet. Innumerable bats, startled at the light, flew on ahead, filling the passage. They were black like the ordinary bat, but with not a few white ones among them. As they followed the stream, little snakes were continuously coiling round their feet; they had to keep cutting and cutting into the stream at these, in order to get on.

Sometimes a rank smell of raw flesh assailed their nostrils and at times they felt sick, but again a delicious heart-soothing fragrance would also come.

The passage gradually widened, and above them something like a transparent column, as it were a pillar of blue ice, was clearly seen. One of the men said that he had heard this kind of stalactite was a mineral from which the Sennin immortals prepare the nectar of immortality – so he had been told.

As they went further, under their feet came the thunder of furious shouts as from a thousand throats of demons fighting. It was terrifying.

Going still further they lit more pine torches, and saw that the place had widened out somewhat. On every side they could see nothing but pitchblack emptiness, but from far and near human cries from time to time arose. Their hearts contracted as at treading the paths of hell.

Now they came to a wide river. There was no indication of the way (no 'miyako-bird' – allusion to Narihira's famous poem). By the sound of it, a torrent was rushing down into an unimaginable abyss. They tested the surging current with their feet, and it was swift as an arrow and colder than any ice – as if it were from the frozen hells Guren and Daiguren.

The further bank was 200–250 feet away, and opposite them there appeared a light something like a blazing torch but not the colour of fire; in the light they described an awe-inspiring form standing in majesty.

Four of the men fell dead then and there. Tadatsune bowed to that spirit, and hearing its voice inwardly, threw the precious sword into the river, upon which the wonderful form disappeared and Tadatsune, his life spared, returned and gave his account.

Shōgun Yoriie, hearing thus about the world within different from this world, determined to send another expedition with many men and a specially made boat. But his senior counsellors dissuaded him, telling him that according to tradition this cave was the abode of the great Bodhisattva of Asama, and from ancient times it had not been permitted to men to look upon it.)

The nyūdō Wada Hidetsura, going to Kenchōji for an interview with master Nanzan (the 20th teacher there), asked about this story of the Cave of Man in the field at the foot of Mount Fuji. The priest said:

'What Your Honour has related is a tale of the heroic daring of warriors. The heroism of Zen must be in penetrating to the uttermost depths of the Cave of Man.

When the aspirant begins his training and enters the Cave of Man in the field of Zen, as he goes further in, he gets a feeling of his feet being cut by icy waters. He experiences sensations of fragrance, and then again there are perceptions of bright light. The treasure sword which he received from his master – there comes a time when he throws it away. When he throws it away, the form of the spirit, which he has been seeing, suddenly vanishes. While yet he sees this spirit form, he is caught by the Buddha, tied up by the dharma, and cannot have the freedom of Zen inspiration. But after the spirit form vanishes, he must go yet one more step into the interior. Do you not hear what I am saying?

> If you want to have the full view of a thousand miles,
> Mount one more storey of the tower.'

TESTS

(1) Going into the Zen cave, there is a feeling of the feet being cut by icy water. Why is that?

(2) Why do sensations appear like a bad smell or a fragrance?
(3) When comes the awareness of bright light?
(4) What is the throwing away of the precious sword?
(5) What is the appearance of the spirit form?
(6) After the spirit form disappears, what is there further within?

(Note by Imai Fukuzan:) The Bushōsōdan records that these tests were used in the interviews of warriors when Kosen Ingen (38th master at Kenchōji) was teaching at Chōjuji temple in Kamakura. They were used when aspirants were entering on the practice of Zen meditation. But in times like the present (1925) when the importance of Zen meditation is overlooked, there will be few who could answer them properly. The fashion of Zen these days, among monks and laymen alike, is to absorb oneself in examining the words of the patriarchs in the kōans, and since they do not experience the states of Zen meditation, there are hardly any who could open their mouths to these tests. The tests have as subject the meditation experiences of a Zen aspirant, experiences of the six consciousnesses (senses plus mind) and then making void the seventh consciousness, and then thrusting a sword down into the heart-field of the eighth Ālaya consciousness. When as at present 'philosophical' followers of Zen hope to travel the path of the patriarchs at high speed on an express train as it were, these kōans are quite unsuitable for them. But twenty or thirty years ago, among some of the senior laymen who practised Zen, there were quite a few who actually went through them.

No. 25. The Nembutsu Robe

The Shōgun Yoriie detested the followers of the Nembutsu (recitation of the name of Amida Buddha in the formula Na-mu-A-mi-da-butsu), and in May 1213 he issued a decree forbidding the recitation. He ordered Yashirō Hiki to investigate travellers, and if he found any priest of the Nembutsu persuasion, to take his robe and burn it. To carry out this order, Yashirō inspected travellers at the side of Mandokoro bridge, and if he found any priest of Nembutsu, he stripped off his robe and burnt it. If he discovered he was breaking the decree banning Nembutsu, he arrested him and threw him into prison.

At this time there was in Ise a Nembutsu follower called Shōnenbō (the Name-reciting priest), and he came to Kamakura and performed the recitation there. Yashirō arrested him and went to burn his robe. Shōnenbō said, 'This robe is the banner of the Three Treasures, it is the holy sign of the sangha, it is the garment of the shadow of all the Buddhas. It is the dress of honour of the Four Guardian Kings and the Eight Dragons. And especially a robe of shōnen (recitation), if it has been an expression of great faith, will not burn even when thrown into a fire.' Yashirō then told his men to throw the robe into the blazing fire. Shōnenbō gave one cry of Namu-Amidabutsu, and the fire went out without burning even the edge of the robe – so it is related.

The priest Sonei approached Master Nanzan with his story, and the teacher said to him, 'Leave this little tale which the followers of the Kamakura Pure Land sect have passed down. Right now before you, when the robe-body is thrown into the fire, how can Shōnenbō save himself? Try a Nembutsu recitation! Prove it to this old teacher.'

Sonei had no words.

TEST
In the blazing fire, how can he save himself? Say something for Sonei.

This became a kōan in Kamakura at the interviews of Yūhō, the 30th master of Zenkōji temple.

No. 26. *Benzaiten of Enoshima*

Doi Yorimune came up to Mizugaoka and visited Mugaku (Bukkō), a general of the Zen sect, and asked about the worship of Benzaiten (goddess of prosperity) of Enoshima Island. He recalled how on the fifth day of the fourth month of the second year of Yōwa (1182), the Minamoto general Yoritomo had been strolling on the beach at Namigoe on the way to Enoshima, and there had met the holy man Bungaku who was a devotee of Benzaiten. He said he would pray for the general's success in arms, and arrangements were made for sacrificial ceremonies, and the erection of a stone torii. This was, he added, really with the motive of exorcizing the curse pronounced by Fujiwara Hidehara (on the Minamotos). He concluded: 'I have brought a picture of the blessing being conferred by Benzaiten.'

The teacher said: 'The Benzaiten prayed to Benzaiten for the military glory of the Minamoto general, and to avert the curse of the other general of those days – is that a male divinity or a female?'

Doi said: 'Whether Benzaiten is a god or a goddess, I do not know. I only know that the form in the picture here is a goddess.'

The teacher said: 'So you go by the form. I suppose you would think that a woman warrior dressed in man's clothes would be a man?'

Doi said: 'Well then, is Benzaiten a male dressed as a female?'

The teacher replied: 'Do you worship Benzaiten as a god or do you worship Benzaiten as a goddess?'

Doi said: 'The reason I worship is nothing to do with whether it is a god or a goddess. I just pray for my welfare.'

The teacher at once caught hold of Doi and rubbed his face, first against the grain of the beard, and then with the grain. Doi did not understand what he meant. The teacher said:

'This fellow! He has never believed in Benzaiten at all. Why does he come here wanting to get approval from me?'

TESTS

(1) Is Benzaiten a god or a goddess? Say!
(2) What did Bukkō mean by rubbing Doi's face with the grain and against the grain? Say!

This incident became a kōan in Kamakura Zen when Issan, the 7th master at Enkakuji, gave it to Sūkō, a mountain hermit.

No. 27. The god Hachiman

After paying a visit to worship at the shrine of Hachiman at Tsurugaoka, Ōba Kagemitsu (a descendant of the Ōba Kageyoshi who had been in charge of the construction of the Hachiman shrine) called at Enkakuji and had an interview with National Teacher Bukkō.

The teacher asked: 'Which way does Hachiman face?'

Kagemitsu said: 'He faces the Great Teacher directly.'

The teacher covered his face with his fan and said: 'How is it now?' *(Imai's note: When the teacher is dead)*

Kagemitsu hesitated.

The teacher snapped the fan shut and hit him on the forehead with it. Kagemitsu had a realization, made a salutation and left.

TEST

How could that blow by Bukkō, Teacher of the Nation, be the occasion of a realization?

This incident was first given as a kōan in Kamakura Zen by priest Nei-issan, 7th master at Enkakuji, to the Ajari (Tendai priest) Hayashi Kōbō Ryōtatsu.

No. 28. *The rite of the wind god at Kamakura*

In the second year of Kangi (1229) there were portents of evil
in the East of Japan. On the sixth day of the seventh month
there was a frost at Kamakura, and at Kanago district in
Musashi province, flakes of snow fell. The diviners searched
the records, to find that in the 39th year of the reign of the
Emperor Kōgen (reigned 214–158 BC) snow had fallen in
June, and there had been a great snowfall in June of the 34th
year of the Empress Suiko (592–628), and another in the
same month of the eighth year of the era called Engi (the
middle part of the reign) of Emperor Daigo (897–930). At
these times there had been a bad year, the people in distress
and fighting breaking out between local gangs. The diviners
gave grave warnings that the omens portended calamities of a
similar nature, with starvation and insurrection. Hōjō Yasutoki
was deeply disturbed. Then an official messenger from Mino
brought a report from headman Makida that a sudden and
intense fall had covered the ground in snow more than a foot
deep.

At this Yasutoki was still more anxious, and he had prayers
said in the great temples to avert disaster, but to no avail, for
the next year in the fifth month, storms and floods continued
for several weeks, and the whole land and everything in it was
in great straits. Yasutoki now had the Esoteric ceremonies for
salvation in crisis performed at all temples, and had the Heart
Sūtra read continuously by the priests at Tsurugaoka Hachiman
shrine. But the force of the wind did not abate.

Then he proposed to perform a sacred rite to the wind god
at the stone torii at Yui-ura; he put the magistrate Yasusada
in charge, and to help him ordered the priest Gyōyū (the
second master of Jufukuji, and also an expert in the Esoteric
Shingon ceremonies, of which he had been a priest before he
entered Zen) to put together a text for the rite.

It happened that Enni Jōza (Zen master Shōichi) was
staying temporarily and teaching Zen at the small temple

Zōkyōin within the Jufukuji temple compound, and he was famous for his Chinese learning. Gyōyū therefore asked him whether he would do it, to which he at once agreed, and taking up the brush, wrote:

> All things are passing,
> Their nature is to arise and end;
> When arising and ending come to an end,
> That Nirvāna is bliss.

Gyōyū looked at this and said doubtfully: 'But this is the verse from the funeral service!'

Enni said: 'We want to have a funeral for the wind devil. Why should we just imitate others when we compose the text for the rite?'

Then Gyōyū and Enni went together, and on the dais of the rite of the wind god, they recited the funeral verse. It is said that the wind immediately changed and dropped.

This is an old Zen story, to engage the idle moment. It is easily misunderstood. Right now, here in these Jewel Deer hills, hurricanes and floods are rising, and our Enkakuji here is on the verge of being overwhelmed! I have to perform the rite of the wind god. Let each one of you bring me a verse with which I can give a funeral to the wind devil.

TESTS

(1) Where does the wind arise from? Say!
(2) Where does the wind devil live? Say!
(3) What does the wind devil look like?
(4) After the funeral, where does the wind devil go back to? Say!
(5) Give me a funeral verse – compose it now!

This first became a Kamakura kōan at the interviews of Kosen, the 29th teacher at Enkakuji.

No. 29.   The one-word charm of Enkakuji

An official who was administrator for Ōkura in the Kamakura district said to the great teacher Mugaku (afterwards Bukkō, Teacher of the Nation):

'In the twelfth month of the fourth year of Jijō (1180), the Minamoto general Raichō planned to build a new palace in Ōkura; Ōba Kageyoshi who was in charge realized that he could not construct a whole new palace in time. So my ancestor, the prefect here, had one very large mansion from within this area which is now the temple compound of Enkakuji, transported to Ōkura to make up the great palace. This edifice was said to have been built originally in Shōryaku times (990), and in those ancient days Abe Yasuaki brushed a protective charm for the preservation of the house. It was nailed to the ridgepole, since when over the centuries it has had no upsets of fortune, and this miraculous protection is spoken of with awe. Today, the great edifice of Enkakuji has been erected, but the ridgepole is still without any charm on it. Would not the great Teacher bless us by writing a charm so that there may never be any disaster to the building?'

It is said that the teacher at once called his attendant Eibin to bring paper and ink, and brushed a single character.

TEST

What character is this charm of one word? Right now present that character to me, let me see it!

This became a kōan in Kamakura Zen in the interviews of Gyokkei, the 52nd master at Enkakuji.

(Imai's note: A good many of the pupils given this kōan present to the teacher words like Buddha, Dharma, God, Water and so on, but none of these is passed. What the word is, is not preserved in the secret scrolls of the Zen sect: let people open the true eye, and see.)

No. 30.   Mirror Zen – Introduction

(Imai's Introduction: At the beginning of the Jōkyū era (1219), fifty days before the fighting broke out, the Nun Shōgun (Hōjō Masako) had a dream of a great mirror floating in the waves off Yui beach, and a voice coming from it: 'I am the voice of the great shrine, and what is to happen in the world is seen in me. There is a war imminent, and the army must be mobilized. If Yasutoki polishes me, he will be victorious and bring about a great peace.' On hearing this dream, Yasutoki sent Hatanojirō Tomosada as an emissary to the great shrine at Yui beach, to pray for the peace of the land.

When the Jōkyū rebellion had been put down, Yasutoki had a mirror made with a circumference of six foot, following the description of the spirit mirror given by the Nun Shōgun of her vision, and it was installed in the shrine of Tsurugaoka Hachiman. Later when Shidō (of the household of Tokimune) founded the Tōkeiji convent-temple, the great mirror was reported to have been moved there and set up in a special mirror hall. But in fighting afterwards between Hōjō Hayagumo and Miura Michisu, the temple was plundered and the mirror carried off: so it is recorded in the Kamakura Journals, Volume 4.

When Enkakuji was burnt down in the seventh year of Ōan (1374), a precious mirror (the one referred to in the first kōan of the present collection), which was one of its treasures, was got away to Tōkeiji, where it was installed in the mirror hall, then enlarged to become the zazen meditation hall for the nuns. Afterwards all the nuns from eastern Japan who entered Tōkeiji did meditation before the mirror, and thus arose Tōkeiji Mirror Zen, as it came to be called. Again it is said that Shidō, the nun who was the founder and first teacher there, had her own realization when facing a mirror, and so the nuns of later generations were following this precedent in meditating facing the great mirror.

The poems which follow are those composed by the

*successive nun teachers at Tōkeiji on the mirror practice.
There were ten of them, but it was the first eight, all by nuns
who had received the full confirmation (inka) of their
realization, that were given as kōans to nuns. The Tests are
those given by Master Sanpaku, the 156th teacher at
Enkakuji, to nuns taking interviews with him. These poems
are the Eight Kōans of the Enkakuji Nuns referred to in
Sōrinzakki.*

The comments (chakugo) here given are those presented by
the nun Myōtō (the widow of Uesugi Yoshimitsu), and they in
turn became subjects presented to nun students. I am not here
recording which Master Sanpaku approved and which he did
not.

In the first year of Keichō (1596) there was a winter retreat
at Tōkeiji attended by 108 nuns, of whom forty-one took
interviews at which they had to present comments to the
kōans. Of these, seventeen were taking one of the ancient
classical kōans, and only eight of these composed poems of
their own as a comment, the others presenting something
from the Zenrin Kushū anthology. There were thirty-five nuns
passed by Master Sanpaku at their interviews, both on their
realization and on their comments, and among them the nun
Myōtei distinguished herself by passing the notoriously
difficult kōan called the Four Katzu!s of Rinzai. There are
accounts of the interviews and the comments given by the
nuns at the interviews, kept in the private archives at Tōkeiji,
but it is not proper to publish such records.

Imai's further comments as given in the appendix:
For many of the Kamakura kōans, some 'comment' or
chakugo was required. Provided that this was a spiritual
utterance manifesting a true expression of Great Realization,
it was not necessary (as it later became necessary) that in
order to pass the kōan some particular Zen phrase had to be
presented. The essential thing was that the words arose from a
great realization. In the comments to the Kamakura Zen
kōans, some saying of the Buddha or of the patriarchs could

be employed if they were infused with life, and again there were poems both classical and newly composed. So long as the comment, whatever its form, did express clearly the realization, the teacher would approve it, and this was the original style of Kamakura Zen. But after the Tenshō era (end of the sixteenth century) gradually quotations from the Zenrin Kushū anthology became more frequent. (This was a collection of over 4,000 put together by the Japanese Zen master Eichō from Chinese Zen texts, for just this purpose.)

A 'comment' to a kōan rises naturally from the inner state on the occasion of realization, and is not something that has to be said in the wake of someone else. Even when a verse is employed by which an ancient expressed this state, it is not now an ancient verse, but one's own. But then there can be some argument as to the particular meaning and appropriateness or otherwise of some of the classical verses, so that in later times it became the rule that at the interviews with the teacher, some particular verse had to be presented in order to be passed through that kōan. So the Zen followers in later centuries came to compile secret Zen records of the ancient comments to particular kōans. Certainly as a means to focus meditations on the comments given by the ancients, and so develop spiritual strength, it was not useless to compile such private collections of the comments given in earlier times.

In the examples which I am venturing to give of comments in the Tōkeiji Mirror Zen, taken from the private records at Tōkeiji, I simply wished to record how in later times, after the sixteenth century, the Zenrin Kushū phrases were used.

The chakugo comments recorded here are taken from the notes of interviews given by Sanpaku, the 156th master at Enkakuji, to nuns of all parts of Eastern Japan who had come to attend a winter retreat on the 350th anniversary of Shidō, founder of Tōkeiji. The comments were given in connection with the Mirror Zen kōans which are recorded below. The records mention whether Master Sanpaku accepted or refused the comments, but I have omitted this here as I am simply giving an example of how the Zenrin Kushū anthology phrases were coming to be used so extensively. (However in some cases, as in the comment in reply to Test 2 of the first poem, two words have been substituted in the Zenrin Kushū lines, to give a completely different meaning – Tr.))

Mirror Zen – the Verses

I   The poem of the founder, the nun Shidō:
If the mind does not rest on anything, there is no clouding,
And talk of polishing is but a fancy.

TESTS

(1) If the mind does not rest on anything, how will anything be seen or heard or known or understood?
Comment: Rising and sinking according to the current, Going and coming, no footprint remains.
(2) A mirror which does not cloud and need no polishing – Set it before the teacher now.
Comment: The things are hidden in no secret treasure-house;
The heart is eternally clear to see.

II   The poem of the second teacher, the nun Runkai:
Various the reflections, yet its surface is unscarred; From the very beginning unclouded, the pure mirror.

TESTS

(1) When it reflects variously, how is it then?
Comment: The heart turns in accordance with the ten thousand things:
The pivot on which it turns is verily in the depths.
(2) If from the very beginning the mirror is unclouded, How is it that there are reflections of karmic obstacles in it?

Comment: Within the pure mirror never clashing with each other,
The reflections of pine and bamboo are in harmony.

(3) Show the pure mirror right before the teacher's face.
Comment: Heaven and earth one clear mirror,
Now as of old, luminous and majestic.

III   The poem of the third teacher, Shōtaku:
As night falls, no more reflections in the mirror,
Yet in this heart they are clearly seen.

TESTS

(1) What does the poem mean?
Comment: On a dark night, things in front of the mirror are seen no more by the eye: yet images are reflected in the heart, and in face of them we go astray. When we have passed beyond this path of illusion, then our gaze pierces through even the darkest night to see the sun-Buddha ever shining everywhere, illumining all.

(2) What is the colour and form of that heart which sees in the dark?
Comment: The ten directions with no sign of an image:
The three worlds pass and leave no trace.

IV   The poem of the fourth teacher, Junsō:
Reflections are clear yet do not touch the eye,
And the I facing the mirror is also forgotten.

TESTS

(1) If you *think* the reflections are there but do not touch the eye, this is at once a dust on the mirror, so what is the meaning? Try and see!
Comment: When it is said that they do not touch the eye, it means that the eye is not joined to awareness: there is no agitation in the heart. So there is not even the thought that they do not touch the eye.

(2) What is the mirror state when I is forgotten?
   To pass this test, the nun had to demonstrate directly
   without recourse to words.

(3) What is the difference between forgetting-I Zen and Void
   Zen (Kū-zen)?
   Comment: Void Zen is still a duality of seeing Voidness in
   the person and in the things. Forgetting-I Zen is the
   Mahayana when mind and its object are one.
   Aspiring to heaven but not seeing heaven;
   Searching for earth but not seeing earth.

V   The poem of the fifth teacher, the former princess Yōdō:
Heart unclouded, heart clouded;
Rising or falling, it is still the same body.

TESTS

(1) Heart unclouded, what is that?
   Comment: Ten thousand miles without a cloud,
   Ten thousand miles of heaven.

(2) Heart clouded, how is that?
   Comment: In the spring, clouds rise round the mountain
   And in the cave it is dark.

(3) What is this rising and falling?
   Comment: The moon sets, and in the pool no reflection;
   A cloud is born and the mountain has a robe.

VI   The poem of the sixth teacher, Ninbō:
Even without any mirror to reflect the things,
Every time one looks, there is a mirror reflecting them in the
heart.

TESTS

(1) What is this looking?

(2) What is this reflecting heart?
   To these tests, the nun was to demonstrate directly without
   words, but many of them did present comments.

73

VII   Poem of the seventh teacher Ryōdō:
If one asks where the reflections in the pure mirror go when
they vanish,
Do you declare their hiding-place.

TEST

Right now this old teacher is asking, where are those
reflections gone? Answer well! Where are they?
Comment: Close the door and shut out the moon,
Dig a well and chisel space apart.

VIII   Poem of the eighth teacher, nun Kanso:
Clouded over from time without beginning is that pure
mirror;
When polished, it reflects – the holy form of Amida.

TESTS

(1) What is this polishing? Speak!
(2) Declare the form of Amida.
After this second test had been passed, a fitting comment
had to be supplied. One such was:
   This body the Lotus Paradise,
   This heart verily Amida.

No. 31.   *The very first Jizō*

Sakawa Koresada, a direct retainer of the Uesugi family,
entered the main hall at Kenchōji and prayed to the Jizō-of-a-
Thousand-Forms there. Then he asked the attendant monk in
charge of the hall:

   'Of these thousand forms of Jizō, which is the very first
Jizō?'

   The attendant said, 'In the breast of the retainer before me
are a thousand thoughts and ten thousand imaginings; which
of these is the very first one?'

No. 11 Polishing and the Buddha appearing in the mirror
(Morikawa)

The samurai was silent.
The attendant said again, 'Of the thousand forms of Jizō,

the very first Jizō is the Buddha-lord who is always using those thousand forms.'

The warrior said, 'Who is this Buddha-lord?'

The attendant suddenly caught him and twisted his nose.

The samurai immediately had a realization.

TESTS

(1) Which is the very first Jizō out of the thousand-formed Jizō?

(2) Which is the very first out of the thousand thoughts and ten thousand imaginings?

(3) What did Koresada realize when his nose was twisted?

This became a kōan at the interviews of Koken, the 61st master at Kenchōji.

No. 32.   The nyo-i sickle of Enkakuji

Ujihira, a steward of the Hōjō Regent, one day visited Enkakuji and told Bukkō about the name Kamakura, which means literally Sickle-store (kama = sickle; kura = store):

> In ancient times, there was born at Hitachi a man named *Kama*tari, and when he was young he went to the capital and served at the palace, where he assisted with great devotion in the great affairs of state. The Emperor Tenchi in the eighth year of his reign (669 AD) gave him the new name of Fujiwara, and his house prospered exceedingly. He undertook a pilgrimage to the shrine of Kashima in Hitachi, and on the way back stopped at the village of Yui in Musashi province, where he had a wonderful dream. As a token he buried a sickle *(kama)* at Matsugaoka of Ō-*kura*, and thereafter the place was called Kama-kura.

No. 12 Hokusai: The war-god Marishi (from India) using bow,
spear, sword and fan with his various arms without
confusion, while balancing on the back of his 'vehicle', a
wild boar. This is to illustrate ki filling the whole body and
each single function without being concentrated to the
detriment of the others. (British Museum)

The teacher said: 'That sickle – where is it now?'

The official said: 'That was all long ago when the place belonged to the great Fujiwaras. No one would go searching for it now.'

The teacher said: 'That sickle has found its way into the main temple at Enkakuji, and I can put my hand on it now.'

The officer drew in his breath with surprise, and asked to see it.

The teacher raised his ceremonial nyo-i metal stick vertically in the air.

Ujihira said: 'But isn't this a nyo-i?'

The teacher: 'This fellow! How is it he can't see the sickle which Lord Fujiwara saw in that dream?'

In the book of the sermons of the master Tōgaku at Enkakuji, it is said that when he presented this as a kōan, he used to say,

'Matsugaoka of Ōkura is not far off; in fact it is here under your feet. Is someone going to bury a sickle here? The sharp edge has never yet been hidden, look! Here it is clearly in front of your very eyes, look! If a spiritual hero can change iron into gold, why hesitate over changing a sickle into a nyo-i?' And he would suddenly produce an old sickle and display it to them – 'Look, look!'

TESTS

(1) That sickle which Lord Fujiwara saw and created in his spirit, where is it now? Say!

(2) Lord Fujiwara's sickle – who made it, and how?

(3) If you see it, say how long and how big it is.

(4) If you can use Lord Fujiwara's sickle, show the receipt for it. Bring the proof!

This was first used as a kōan at the interviews of Tōgaku, the 61st master at Enkakuji.

No. 33. *The cat-monster*

When Odawara Castle fell to the attackers in the Meiō period (the end of the fifteenth century), Akiko, who had been a maid in the service of Mori Fujiyori, the lord of the castle, escaped with a cat which had been her pet for years. She took refuge in the villa of the painter Takuma at Kinokubo by the Nameri River. She lived there some years, and then the cat became a wild supernatural monster which terrorized the people, finally even preying on infants in the village.

The local officials joined with the people in attempts to catch it, but with its strange powers of appearing and disappearing, the swordsmen and archers could find nothing to attack, and men and women went in dread day and night.

Then in December of the second year of Eishō (1505), priest Yakkoku went up on to the dais at Hōkokuji and drew the picture of a cat, which he displayed to the congregation with the words:

'As I have drawn it, so I kill it with a Katzu!, that the fears may be removed from the hearts of the people.'

He gave the shout, and tore to pieces the picture of the cat.

On that day a woodcutter in the valley near the Takuma villa heard a terrible screech; he guided a company of archers to the upper part of the valley, whre they found the body of the cat-monster, as big as a bear-cub, dead on a rock. The people agreed that this had been the result of the master's Katzu!

TESTS

(1) How can tearing up a picture with a Katzu! destroy a living monster?

(2) That devil-cat is right now rampaging among the people, bewitching and killing them. Kill it quickly with a Katzu! Show the proof!

(Imai's note: This is an exercise in the Katzu!)

This became a kōan in Kamakura Zen at the interviews of Unei, the 174th master at Kenchōji.

No. 34. *The destruction of the toad at Kaizōji*

During the regency, in the twenty-third year of Ō-ei (1316), Uesugi Ahonokami Norizane retired, on the fifth day of the eighth month, to Shirai Castle in his domain in Kamakura, to mourn for Ashikaga Mochiuji (for whose life, though an enemy, he had pleaded). At the same time Uesugi retainers, apprehending danger to themselves in the troubled times, left Kamakura and dispersed in many places in Izu and other regions, with a good number of them also renouncing home to become students at the temples of Kamakura. Now Suwako, one of Uesugi's favourite concubines, had fallen in love with Iwai Hanzo Kaneshige (an official at Kaizōji temple). Because of this affair, she did not wish to go to Shirai Castle with her lord. She suddenly appeared at Kaizōji, and in an agony of frustration, stabbed herself. Kaneshige, fearful that the whole circumstance would come to light, buried her at night under the Buddha hall of the temple. It was said that afterwards she became changed into a great toad which sucked out life from living things, and this became known as one of the ten ghost stories of Kamakura.

Now about this time it was found that the few fawns which were born each year from the white deer at Enkakuji, after the departure of the Uesugis began to die within two or three days. So one year the monk who was in charge of the accounts at the temple went to see the birth, which was always in the White Deer Grotto. When he looked, he saw at the back of the cave a great toad, crouching as if it were sucking up something, and the baby deer seemed as if falling into unconsciousness. They gradually weakened and died. Then he remembered the stories that had been going round, about a weird toad that had the power of sucking out the life from living things. He rushed at it and chased it till it disappeared under the floor of the Buddha Hall of Kaizōji, where its tracks suddenly came to an end.

At the time, in the Kamakura area many new-born children had been dying within two or three days of birth, and there was always an appearance in the house just after the birth of an uncanny toad, which appeared and then disappeared under the floor. Sometimes people had managed to find a track, which they followed until in every case it disappeared under the floor of the Buddha Hall of Kaizōji. So Morikawa Michiyoshi (an official for the area) came to Kaizōji and conducted a search under the floor of the Buddha Hall. There was no trace of the giant toad, but they discovered a place where there was a mound of earth; when this was opened up they came to a coffin containing the remains of the body of a woman dressed in beautiful robes and golden hairpins. Then Sōetsu (who was in charge of affairs concerned with lay people) was ordered to arrange a funeral ceremony to exorcize the toad, but its visitations continued as before. Morikawa reported this to the authorities, who thereupon arranged a prayer ceremony to be performed by the priests of the Hachiman shrine, but again without effect.

Then an official request was made to priest Jikin (namely Ketsugan, the 126th master at Kenchōji) to conduct a service of prayer for the destruction of the witch-toad. Accordingly on the eighth day of the third month of the 29th year of Ōei, under the chairmanship of Hosokawa Hidetsugu, the ceremony was organized, and when the public had assembled, the priests of all the Kamakura temples were ranged in their ceremonial ranks in the main hall for the service. Jikin however came by himself to Kaizōji, and without coming to the main hall, went straight to the Buddha hall. Glaring, he shouted the word 'Kan!' (frontier-gate) at the top of his voice, and then declared to them: 'The service today is over; do not make the offerings of incense, do not read the sūtras, but go back to your temples.'

Thereafter there were no more visitations of the toad, and the people of the region were at peace.

TESTS

(1) What is the meaning of the word Kan!? Say!
(2) What is the virtue in that one word Kan!? Say!
(3) What was the real meaning of shouting Kan! and terminating the service?

This incident became a kōan of Kamakura Zen at the interviews of Unei, the 174th master at Kenchōji.

No. 35.   *The Kannon at Hase*

Miura Nobuto, naval commander at Hase, had practised Zen for a long time. He happened to mention to the teacher Hakudō, when he met him on the occasion of a ceremony of confession and absolution at Hōkokuji temple, that the Kannon at Hase was a great figure over ten feet high.

The teacher said, 'What is the difference in weight between Your Honour and Kannon?'

The commander said, 'The weight is the same.'

The teacher: 'Your Honour is just over five feet tall. How can your weight be the same as Kannon over ten feet?'

The commander: 'The weighing was done before I was born.'

The teacher: 'I'm not asking about before you were born. What is it now?'

The commander: 'By the power of meditation on Kannon, the weight comes out the same.'

TESTS

(1) How can the weights be compared before birth?
(2) What really is this saying that with his present body of

82

just over five feet his weight is the same as the ten-foot
Kannon?
(3) What is this about the power of meditation of Kannon?

This began to be used as a kōan in the interviews of Kohō, the
72nd teacher at Kōzenji.

No. 36.   *Yakushi of a thousand forms*

On the eighth day of the eleventh month of the first year of
Katei (1235) General Yoritsune was in great pain from an
infected wound. All shrines and temples were to offer prayers
for him, and the Buddhist image-maker Yasusada was
ordered to make, in a single night, a Yakushi of a thousand
forms, each one to be 1 ft 6 ins (Yakushi is the bodhisattva of
healing). And the astrologer Chikamoto was to perform a
ceremony 36,000 times in the same time. It is said that in the
event, the general recovered in less than a day.
  I don't ask you about the 36,000 ceremonies, but how
could the thousand images of Yakushi be made in a single
night?

TEST
Those in the line of the patriarchs are said to have the
ability to use a thousand hands and a thousand eyes. Now
use them to make the Yakushi of a thousand forms in an
instant. Bring the proof of it and show me!

This was first given as a kōan to the Buddhist image-maker
Yasunori by Zen master Daien (the 3rd teacher at Enkakuji).
*(Note by Imai Fukuzan: This story of the Buddhist image-
maker Yasusada and how at the official order he made the
Yakushi of a thousand forms in a single night appears in a
number of writings. There is a matter-of-fact explanation
according to which it could be done easily. At that time what*

*was done to make a Yakushi of a thousand forms as a prayer
for recovery from illness was, to impress a black-ink stamp
with the holy picture on to a board and then cut up the latter
into sections each with one of them on it. After the ceremony,
many of them were thrown into the river. Again there was,
and still is, a custom of making seal impressions on to pieces
of paper in the same way. Yasusada would have had a number
of apprentices and it would have been nothing marvellous for
them to turn out a thousand Yakushi representations in one
night perhaps each one making a hundred or so.*

*But from the point of view of Zen training, as the wording
of the test shows, the Zen pupil has to display his skill with a
thousand hands and a thousand eyes. If he cannot do that,
then however many times he repeats a dhāranī or mantra of
the bodhisattva of a thousand hands and eyes, he will not be
sure whether it has any effect or not. And then he might as
well give up his dazed mumbling and go.*

*This is something the Zen student has to meditate on. If he
becomes one who can use the thousand eyes and hands freely,
he will be able to make not merely the Yakushi of a thousand
forms, but the three thousand Buddhas of whom they speak
at the ordination ceremony, in an instant. If he cannot do it,
he may make the Yakushi of a thousand forms, he may pray
for recovery from illness, but what will be the use? The one
who knows, he alone knows.)*

No. 37. The snake at Itōzaki

*(Imai's note: In the third volume of the Chronicles of Nine
Generations of the Hōjō Rulers is the following story:*

On the first day of the sixth month of the third year of
Kennin (1203 AD) General Yoriie was stopping at a
hunting lodge in a remote part of Izu. In the mountains at a
place called Itōzaki there is a great cave. Lord Yoriie felt

that there was something strange within it, and Wada Heitarō ordered a warrior named Tanenaga to investigate the interior. Tanenaga took a pine-torch and went into the cave. He was there from the hour of the snake (10 a.m.) till the hour of the bird (6 a.m.), when he came out and reported.

Within the cave he had gone along several leagues. The darkness was indescribable. Holding high the pine-torch he went far in; in places there was a little stream flowing. On each side were slabs of rock, and the damp underfoot was slippery. Going still further, he came on a great snake lying coiled up. It was about a hundred feet long, with two glittering eyes and layers of scales with moss growing on them. When it saw Tanenaga, it opened its mouth wide and made to swallow him. He drew his sword and cut through the mouth lengthwise, so that it was split apart, and the snake fell dead, shaking the earth. Its huge body blocked the way further in, and he gave up and returned.

The Shōgun was displeased with this report, saying that to go into the cave without exploring it right to the end had no value. Wada Heitarō was mortified and Tanenaga slunk away.

This is the account in the Hōjōkudaiki; it appears in more detail in the Kamakura Ezōshi (picture-book), and in Kantō Ghost Stories, in which it is the third.)

Once Banda Moritsuna, when seeing priest Tōri, the 16th teacher at Kenchōji, brought up the story of the slaying of the Itōzaki snake. Tōri pointed to himself and said:

'And this old general too is displeased that it was merely killing a snake and not penetrating the inner depths of that cave. Though a snake of the three poisons and five passions be cut down, unless the inner depths are penetrated, the real essence of Zen cannot be known. Far within, where the snakes of the three poisons and five passions are gathered, is a dark cavern of the basic Ignorance, and here the magician-king manipulates at will his 84,000 retainers. Unless your one sword cuts him into two, your world will not be at peace. Already you have spent tens of years polishing that one sword; you do cut into the crowd of sins in the outer cave, but you have not struck down the devil in the inmost cavern of Ignorance. And so at the door of the prison of life-and-death, you are still under his spell.'

Moritsuna said: 'Your Reverence has told us that in the way of the patriarchs there is no life-and-death. Why do you now teach about the door of its prison?'

The teacher said: 'The golden coin comes from out of the iron-black mountain of Pamir. Get to the bottom of that line.'

TESTS

(1) Why is it taught: In the line of the patriarchs, no life-and-death?

(2) When you break down the prison door, how is it then?

(3) What is at the bottom of the line: The golden coin comes from out of the iron-black mountain?

This was first used as a kōan at the interviews of Gukei, the 63rd teacher at Enkakuji.

No. 38. Bukkō's age

Priest Mugaku (later called Bukkō Kokushi) was fifty-six when he came to Kamakura and founded Enkakuji. With his white hair and old face, he looked like one who had passed the seventieth year.

The saint Jōnen heard it said that the old priest was only in his fifties, and hesitantly asked him how old he was.

The teacher replied, 'The same as Amida.'

The saint said, 'Why, how old is Amida?'

The teacher said, 'Amida is the same age as the saint before me. If the saint knows the origin of the true life of himself, he will realize the Buddha's age, and will know how many years is this old monk.'

TESTS

(1) Setting aside the teacher's age, setting aside the Buddha's age, at this instant what is the origin of your own true life?

(2) Amida Buddha is called the Tathāgata of eternal ages. How about you?

(3) Forget for a little the teacher's age – do you know the age of this old monk before you?

This incident began to be used in the interviews given by Butsuju (literally 'Buddha-age'), the 21st teacher at Enkakuji.

No. 39.   *The birth of the Buddha*

Ishida Yamato-no-kami entered upon the Way at Enkakuji, where he had the Zen interviews with Ikka, who was the 124th teacher there. One day he asked the teacher, 'In the scriptures which I have been reading since I began here, there are various different teachings about the day of the Buddha's birth. Which day of which month is the right one?'

The teacher said, 'Don't talk about different teachings. When you see the nature to be Buddha, that is the birth of the World-honoured One.'

TESTS

(1) If you say, See the nature to be Buddha, immediately a snake with two heads appears. Are the nature and the Buddha the same or different? If the same, why does it have to tell you to see the nature to be Buddha? If there is a difference, say wherein it is, that seeing the nature is something separate from being Buddha.

No. 13 Master Butsuju

(2) What is that you recognize when you talk about the
    nature being Buddha? Say!

This became a Kamakura kōan in the interviews of Gyokkei,
the 131st teacher at Enkakuji.

No. 40. · *'The world-honoured one has been born!'*

Uesugi Masayoshi entered training at Meigetsuin, and the
teacher set him the kōan of the birth of the Buddha. A little
after one year, Masayoshi had a realization during the
Rōhatsu training week, and shouted, 'The World-honoured
Buddha is born!' Then he took a few steps forward and cried
loudly, 'In heaven above and earth below I alone am the
honoured one!'

   The teacher said, 'Tradition tells:
            that the World-honoured One was twelve months in
              the womb,
            that he was born from the right side of his mother,
            that he took seven steps and then uttered his great cry.

How did you come out? Say, say! If you cannot say, it is no
Buddha that has been born but a fox-spirit making a false
appearance.'

            Masayoshi said:
            'I entered my home and conformed to it,
            I followed the karma and conformed to it,
            I trod on the head of Vairochana.'
            The teacher: 'What is this treading?'
            Masayoshi: 'The holiest One is not in the first six
              steps.'

TESTS

(1) What was the World-honoured One doing in the twelve months in the womb? Say!
(2) Why was the World-honoured One born from the right side? Say!
(3) A baby might take just one or two steps, or it might take eight or nine steps. Why is it taught that there were just the seven steps? Say! (To solve the third question, you have to understand what Masayoshi said.)

This was first used as a kōan in the interviews of Daien, the 166th teacher at Enkakuji.

No. 41. *The flower hall on Buddha's birthday*

The nun Myōan of Tōkeiji practised Zen in interviews with Tanei, the 74th teacher at Enkakuji, who set her as kōans the poems composed by Yōdō (5th abbess of Tōkeiji and a former princess) and her attendants. These poems were on the theme of gathering and arranging the flowers on the birthday of the Buddha. The poem of Yōdō is:

> Decorate the heart of the beholder,
> For the Buddha of the flower hall
> Is nowhere else.

TESTS

(1) By what do you recognize the heart of the beholder?
(2) Say how you would decorate the flower hall.
(3) If it is to worship a Buddha who is nowhere else than in the heart, then what do you want with a flower hall? Say!

The poem of Ika, a former court lady is:

> Throw away into the street the years of the past.
> What is born instead, on the flower dais,
> Let it raise its new-born cry.

90

No. 14 Princess Yōdō, fifth abbess of Tōkeiji
(International Society for Educational Information, Tokyo)

TESTS
(1) When the years have been thrown away, what is it that is born in their place?
(2) Let this teacher here and now listen to the new-born cry.
(3) Where is the flower dais?

The poem of the nun Myōkō is:

> Born, and forgetting the parents who bore it –
> The parents who are Shaka and Amida.

TESTS

(1) What does the poem mean?
(2) Where is the birth?
(3) Where are Shaka and Amida?
(4) Speak a word of when parents and child come face to face.

The poem of the nun Atoku, another of the attendants, is:

> Coming out from the Buddha-womb
> To become myself,
> Now let it ring out – the Dharma's new-born cry!

TESTS

(1) What is it like in the Buddha-womb?
(2) Let the Dharma's new-born cry ring out.

(*Imai's note: Master Tanei used these poems of Yōdō and her attendants, sung by them on the birthday festival of the Buddha on April 8, as kōans for the nuns of Tōkeiji. And in the Kamakura temples generally, these and other kōans on everyday things were given first to novices and nuns who had scanty literary attainments, before any classical Chinese kōan.*)

No. 42. Sermon

The head monk at Hōkokuji temple was deaf and could not hear the preaching of the Dharma. He asked to take charge of the sūtras as librarian, and for more than ten years he perused them. But he found that the accounts of the Buddha's life in the various sūtras did not agree, and he asked Abbot Hakudō, the fifth master of the temple, which was right. The Abbot said, 'What is in the sūtras is as a finger pointing to the moon or a net to catch fish. What is a Zen man doing muddying his mind with sūtra-phrases and inferences about various teachings and wanting to know which is right and which is wrong? The head monk's practice is itself the Buddha's practice; when the head monk left home that was itself the Buddha's leaving home. When the head monk attained the Way, that was itself the Buddha's attaining the Way. When the head monk enters Nirvāna, that is the Buddha entering Nirvāna. The head monk has already left home and is far advanced in the Way, but has not yet entered Nirvāna; he is today in the stage of the forty-nine years of preaching. Now, for the sake of men and heaven and the ten thousand beings, let him try giving a sermon. Attention all!'

The kōan: Say what sermon it is that the great ones of the Sangha give as their sermon for men and heaven!

TESTS

(1) You are giving your sermon in the high heaven-world, and now you rise to the world of no form. To that which has no colour or form, what is your sermon? Say!

(2) In heaven when you are told to face the Brahma-king, how do you make your sermon? Say!

(3) You rise to the skies and come to the heaven of Maitreya and enter the palace of Maitreya – how will be your sermon? Say!

(4) You go to the heaven on Meru, and you are invited to take the Dharma-seat of Jizō. How will you make your sermon? Say!

(5) You enter the dragon palace in the ocean. For the eight Dragon Kings, how will be your sermon? Say!

(6) A man comes and asks you to give a sermon to a baby less than a month old. How do you make the sermon? Say!

(7) There is a deaf old man of over a hundred. You are asked to give a sermon, but he cannot hear anything of ·the teaching because of his deafness. To this deaf man, how do you make the sermon? Say!

(8) There is a furious brigand, who as yet has no belief in the Three Treasures of Buddhism, and in the middle of the night he comes to your room, waves a naked sword over your head and demands money. If you have nothing to give him, your life will be cut off by his sword. For this man what will your sermon be? Say!

(9) A foreign enemy invades our country, killing and plundering. When this man comes and you are asked to give him the Sermon For The Brigand, you do not know his foreign language. At this moment what will you do to make your sermon? Say!

(10) You are face to face with death, your life is running out, you can hardly breathe and cannot open your mouth. Then a man asks you for a sermon on entering Nirvāṇa. By what means do you make your sermon? Say!

(11) You enter hell. When you preach a sermon for Emma-Ō the judge of the dead, how will you teach then? Say!

(12) The beings in hell are night and day screaming in pain and have no time to hear the teaching. To those on the sword-mountain, to those in the blood-lake, how will you give a sermon? Say!

(13) You are born in the paradise of the Pure Land. With what sermon will you glorify the holy teachings of Amida? Say!

(14) When you are asked to give the sermons of the Buddha's forty-nine years preaching in one word, how will your sermon be? Say!

(*Imai's note: the main kōan began to be used as such in Kamakura Zen with the 13th master of Hōkokuji temple. When he put his disciples under the hammer with his kōan, he always made them go through all the fifteen questions, and in the*

Bukedōshin records they are called the Fifteen Gates of Hōkokuji.

A doctor attached to the Bakufu government put up a notice at the great gate of Hōkokuji which said:

Though you pass the five gates of Hōkokuji, there are fifteen gates still to pass in the Master's interview room.

The Sōrin-zakki miscellaneous records state that when young monks came to Hōkokuji seeking lodging for a night, they were first presented with these fourteen questions, and if they could meet one of them properly, they were allowed to stay.)

No. 43.   The source of heaven

In the first year of Shō-an (1299) Priest Ka-ō built at Kenchōji the Tengen (Source of Heaven) retreat. On the day of the ridgepole raising, the Lord of Tango, Koremasa, came to see it, and he said,

'I hear that the retreat has been named Source of Heaven. But is there any source from which comes heaven itself?'

'There is, there is,' said the priest; 'does Your Grace wish to see it?'

The nobleman said, 'Then I ask you to show me.'

The priest caught hold of him, and picking up a block of wood, hit him on the crown of the head with it twice. The nobleman had a realization from the blow, and said,

'By your grace this old knight could go beyond the thirty-three heavens and reach their source.'

TESTS

(1) Where is the way to the source of heaven?
(2) What is the meaning of the two blows on the crown of the head? If it is just a means to enlighten another, one would do, or three, or four, or thirty would be all right. Why did Priest Ka-ō hit the Lord of Tango just twice?

This became a kōan in Kamakura Zen at the interviews of Daikō, the 81st master at Kenchōji.

No. 44. *Wielding the spear with hands empty*

(Imai's note: Nanjo Masatomo, a master of the spear, was at Kenchōji to worship, and afterwards spoke with priest Giō about using a spear on horseback. Giō said, 'Your Honour is indeed well versed in the art of the spear. But until you have known the state of wielding the spear with hands empty, you will not penetrate to the ultimate secret of the art.' Nanjo said, 'What do you mean?' The teacher said, 'No spear in the hands, no hands on the spear.' The spear master did not understand. The teacher said further, 'If you don't understand, your art of the spear is a little affair of the hands alone.')

In December of 1256 Fukuzumi Hideomi, a government official, was given the kōan 'wielding the spear with hands empty'. He wrestled furiously with this without being able to attain the state, and one evening he paced to and fro many times between the outer hall of Kenchōji and the approach to the teacher's room, until he was exhausted. He quietly crept into a little grotto near the hall, and repeated again and again 'empty hands, empty hands (kara-te, kara-te)'. However a monk who was doing a punishment sitting (to sit all night in meditation posture for having broken a monastery rule) overheard Hideomi when in his meditation he said 'kara-te, kara-te', and thought it was 'kane-dase, kane-dase (give some money, give some money)'. He thought it was a robber and raised the alarm. The priest with the office of jikijitsu and others made a quick search round the hall, and caught Hideomi.

At that time Hideomi was very ill with tuberculosis of the lungs, and moreover in his absorption with the kōan, he had forgotten to eat for several days, so that his flesh was wasted and his bones weak, and his body on the verge of death. The jikijitsu Chikō hit him on the back and said, 'Let not this heart be set on any place', and gave a Katzu! shout.

Hideomi nodded, and then quietly died.

TESTS
(1) How is it, to wield a spear with hands empty?
(2) What has the phrase about not setting the heart got to do with the empty hands kōan?

This became a kōan with the interviews of Kosen, the 38th teacher at Kenchōji.

No. 45. The Kenchōji library

In the 15th year of Eishō (1519) the Lord of Odawara, Hōjō Nagashi, was enlarging the famous Nirayama library at Izu. Desirous of enlarging the stock of books also, he had requests made to the Five Mountains and Ten Sects (i.e. the Zen temples) of Eastern Japan. Accordingly in the October of that year an emissary, Tomita Jūrōkoresada, came with instructions to ask the number of rare manuscripts at Kenchōji. The abbot Unei, the 174th holder of the office, told him, 'This temple has a store of 100,000 scrolls; if you examine them, you will be able to know absolutely everything about the affairs of gods, Buddhas, and men.'

The emissary was amazed. Then he happily reported to the librarians at Nirayama. At the time it was known that the Kenchōji library was the poorest of the libraries at Kamakura (*because many MSS had been lost in a fire in 1293 – Tr.*), so that among the seniors of the three classes (scholars, administrators, and librarians) there were many who were suspicious of what Unei had said.

The next month, November, ten officers of the library arrived and said, 'The library of our Lord does not come up to

10,000 MSS. If you are now holding 100,000 scrolls, it is several times what your old library possessed and is certainly a great increase. To make a copy of 100,000 MSS would be no easy thing. Therefore today we request that first of all we should make a rough calculation of the number of characters in the rare works here, so that we can estimate the amount of copying necessary. Please therefore let us look over the scrolls.'

The abbot said: 'The 100,000 scrolls have only one character on them; why should you need to count the characters?'

The emissary said: 'What is this one character?'

The abbot said: 'This one character is not loyalty and not disloyalty, not filial piety and not filial impiety, not good and not not-good, not bad and not not-bad, not god and not not-god, not Buddha and not not-Buddha, not heart and not not-heart. How should copying be needed of this character, when all beings from birth, day and night, with every thought, are writing this character?'

The emissary replied: 'Your Reverence told us previously that if one examined the 100,000 scrolls, one would be able to know absolutely everything about the affairs of gods, Buddhas and men. How could you say this?'

The priest said: 'I could say it because the 10,000 things of the world all arise from this one character.' The official said: 'Why is this character written to fill 100,000 scrolls?' The abbot spread all ten fingers and danced in front of him.

TESTS

(1) How do you copy this character? Say!
(2) How is it that this character is written to fill 100,000 scrolls? Say!
(3) What did Unei really mean by his dancing? Say!

This incident became a kōan at the interviews of Kochū, 140th master of Enkakuji.

No. 46. *Sameness*

In the first year of Shunyu (1241) of the Southern Sung Dynasty, priest Rankei (afterwards Zen Master Daikaku) came to a desire to carry Zen to the east; and in March, with five attendants (Giō, Ryōsen, Ryūkō, Taimon, Kotsugo) he set sail to the east for Hizen (present-day Nagasaki). But when they were passing the coast off Shantung they encountered a typhoon which sank their boat. They managed to transfer to the ship (Hachiman) which was making the same voyage, and in the 4th year of Kangen (1247), on the twenty-fourth day of the seventh month, they arrived at Hakata in Kyūshū.

(On the first boat) going east to Hizen, when the boat was being driven along by a raging wind and spun round its length by the furious waves, the passengers were terrified, and many had an aspect like death. Rankei was saying again and again 'Sameness, sameness' (Hinten, hinten – the Japanese approximation to the P'ing-têng of his Szechuan dialect). 'When you put the mind in Sameness with the boat, even if it overturns, that will not trouble you; when you put your mind in Sameness with the waves, even sky-high breakers will not frighten you; when you put your mind in Sameness with life-and-death, there will be no grieving after the body; when the subject comes to Sameness of mind with the lord, the country is at peace; when the child comes to Sameness with the parents, the family is happy; when the husband comes to Sameness with the wife, their association is perfect; when living beings come to Sameness of mind with the Buddha, delusive passions come to an end. When the Buddha has sameness of mind with living beings, there appear compassion and virtue. To come to the samādhi of Sameness when approaching or leaving any thing great or small is what I mean by Bringing-everything-to-One.'

TESTS

(1) How do you come to Sameness right now? Say!

(2) In the ocean of life and death, the boat of the four great elements (the body) meets a typhoon, and is about to capsize. At that moment, with what do you come to Sameness? Say!

(3) You are sitting in profound meditation when a blazing fire comes towards you and you cannot escape. With what then do you come to Sameness? Say!

(4) You are sitting in deep meditation when a ruffian comes at you to attack you. If you become like him in Sameness of mind, you too will be a ruffian. In such a case how do you understand the real Sameness of mind? Say!

This became a kōan in Kamakura Zen in the interviews of Master Kosen.

No. 47.   *The badger-headed Kannon*

At Enkakuji there was an old badger which lived for many years under the Kannon Hall of the temple complex near the lotus lake by the outer gate. It was an expert in the badger's traditional art of bewitching passers-by, and the local people called the area in front of the main gate of Enkakuji 'Badger's Way'.

In the first year of Ōei (1394), Hōjō Ujitsune (of Odawara Castle) had completed the building of a splendid temple at the foot of Mt Hakone, and he earnestly requested Priest Iten (Abbot of Daitokuji) to come from Kyōto to consecrate it. At the same time he invited all the dignitaries and Zen followers of the Kamakura Zen temples, great and small, to add to the solemnity of the occasion. He hoped that the magnificence of the temple would redound to the greater prestige and power of the lord of Odawara.

In March of that year, his emissary Tawara Yoshichika went round with the invitations, and having delivered theirs to Enkakuji, took his leave about four o'clock in the afternoon to go on to Kenchōji. But on the way, his party of eight warriors was enchanted by the badger, so that though in broad daylight, it seemed to them as if they were in darkness; they became completely confused and unable to advance or make any progress. They noticed the light of a farmhouse and made towards it, but there was no answer from within. They shouted and beat on the door several times, whereupon the door pillars suddenly collapsed and some of them were injured. When the envoy awoke from the spell he saw with amazement that the sun was only beginning to set behind the hills in the west, and realized that evening had not yet come. In front of them on the river bank was only a single horse stall. He realized that this was what they had seen as a farmhouse: when they hammered on the door, they had punched the horse's rump, and the injuries to some of them had been not from collapse of the front pillars, but from kicks of the horse's hooves.

The envoy was furious, and ordered the local prefect to have the badger hunted down, and a party of swordsmen and archers was accordingly dispatched to Enkakuji. But in the daytime they could not find any traces of it, and when they searched at night, they fell under its spell, and were unable to catch and kill it. The officials finally in despair at their fruitless efforts ordered Enkakuji to track down the old badger.

On the first day of the fourth month of the first year of Ōei, Abbot Ekihō of Enkakuji dressed himself as a layman (for the badger avoided priests) and came out of the gate. The cherry tree on the right side of the lotus lake suddenly came into flower, and under it was a beautiful girl, who filled a bowl with wine and offered it to him. The master shook his whole body and gave a tremendous Katzu! shout, on which there was a great earthquake, and the old badger fell dead.

The next morning this was reported to the prefectural office. The priests of Hachiman, fearing that the town people might be haunted by the vengeful spirit of the badger, made a

Kannon with a badger's head, and installed it on the Badger's Way, next to the Horse-headed Kannon, and it was called by the local people Badger Bodhisattva.

The nun Myōjun of Tōkeiji convent-temple made a poem in praise of the Badger Bodhisattva:

> Should we refuse to call the Bodhisattva, 'Badger'?
> It is Kannon who by magic changes men into Buddhas.

TESTS

(1) Right now I have become an old badger: do you try a Katzu! to save me.

(2) Right now try changing those men who have become badgers into Buddhas.

(3) When the badger head is put on Kannon, does the badger become Kannon or Kannon become the badger? Say!

This incident became a kōan in Kamakura Zen in the interviews of Keisho the 153rd master at Enkakuji.

No. 48. *The basic truth of Buddhism*

A knight of Ōfuna and a student of Zen, Kōno Sadakuni, who was avoided by people because of his hasty temper, once came to Master Setsuō, the 25th master at Kenchōji temple, and shouted at the top of his voice:

'What is the basic truth of Buddhism?' The teacher told his attendant to light the stove, and said, 'Come nearer, come nearer.'

The knight again asked, 'The basic truth of Buddhism – what is it?'

The teacher beckoned to the attendant to serve him with tea and cakes.

He asked again: 'The basic truth of Buddhism – what is it?' The teacher told the attendant to serve him rice.

Then the knight said, 'I thank you indeed for your so courteous hospitality. But unfortunately I have still not been told what is the basic truth of Buddhism.'

The Master said: 'The basic truth of Buddhism is nothing other than this. When freezing, to make warm; when parched, to drink; when famished, to eat; when exhausted, to sleep. This is all out in the open before you, with not a speck of anything doubtful. It is the basic truth of spiritual impulse and action, and if the knight has the seeing eye, he will find it underlying everything I do, walking or standing or sitting or lying down.'

The knight thanked him and left. Outside, he said to the attendant: 'When I asked the teacher just now about the basic truth of Buddhism, he showed it with fire in the stove, with tea and cakes, and finally with boiled rice. But suppose I met him on the road, and asked him about the basic truth of Buddhism, what would he show it with then?'

The attendant said, 'Leaving the teacher for the moment, *I* should wave my hands and move my feet to show the basic truth of Buddhism.'

The knight said, 'Even if I have a seeing eye, suppose you cannot make use of either hand or foot or mouth or nose when I ask what is the basic truth of Buddhism, what will you show it with then?'

The attendant was silent.

TEST
Bring a word for the attendant.

This incident became a kōan in Kamakura Zen at the interviews of Isei, the 156th master at Kenchōji.

No. 49. *The divine snake of the Benten shrine*

In the first year of Shōan (1299), on the occasion of the

festival of the guardian divinity of the Kenchōji precinct, the Zen student Ota Yorikatsu paid a visit to Kenchōji and made an offering at the shrine of Benten (or Benzaiten, goddess of prosperity, also the guardian divinity). He conceived a desire to see the divine snake, which was the traditional form taken by the guardian spirit, and asked the senior priest Daishun where it was to be seen.

The priest said: 'Kenchōji has never never concealed the divine snake form of Benzaiten; it is displayed clearly before the eyes of all. I only ask you to try opening that true eye which can see the form of the divine snake coiled round this humble priest, which protects the temple, and has never never left us. This old priest is day and night holding that snake to himself, and receiving from it blessings without end.'

TESTS

(1) Do you feel that divine snake right now coiled round your body and protecting the temple? Say!
(2) When you hold to yourself the divine snake of Benzaiten, what is the blessing you are receiving right now? Say!

This incident was first given as a kōan in Kamakura Zen at the interviews of Sekishitsu, the 43rd master of Kenchōji.

No. 50.   Reading one's own mind

A mountain hermit, Jōkai of Suwa in Shinano Province, made a visit to Zenkōji and had an interview with priest Kohō. He said: 'I have been living on Mount Mitake in Shinano for twenty years practising the arts of the mountain hermits, and now I can easily boil sand and turn it into rice.'

The teacher said: 'And I have been living here in this temple for twenty years practising the way of the alchemists of India, and now I can easily take up iron and turn it into gold.'

The hermit picked up one of the iron rods used as tongs in

the stove and handed it to the teacher, saying, 'Let us see you turn this to gold.'

The teacher at once took the hermit's hand and pulled it on to the iron pot on the stove, saying, 'Instead of my taking the iron and turning it to gold, let us boil you and turn you to rice. Your narrow obstinacy is harder than iron, and if we don't do that first, I won't be able to turn it to gold.'

The hermit was impressed and went out, but came back the next day to say, 'I have noticed in looking over your Buddhist sūtras that there are six supernormal powers in Buddhism (flying, thought-reading etc.). Can you yourself exercise these powers?'

It happened that a pheasant in the garden gave a cry, and the teacher pointed at it and said, 'Even this golden pheasant is exercising them – every time he flies.'

The hermit said: 'I don't mean that sort of power. Do you for instance have the power to read the mind of others?'

The teacher said: 'You should first find out about reading your own mind. If you can't read your own mind, how will you ever be able to read the mind of others?'

The hermit said: 'What is this reading one's own mind?'

The teacher said: 'An eight-sided grindstone whirling in empty space.'

TESTS

(1) What is the method of taking iron and turning it to gold?
(2) Is reading one's own mind and reading the mind of others the same thing or different?

This incident became a kōan in Kamakura Zen at the interviews of Kohan Shūshin of the Ōbai subtemple at Enkakuji.

No. 51.   The dharma-interview of Nun Mujaku

In the Shōshūsan traditions it is said that the nun Mujaku, before she had been ordained, used to visit the teacher Daiye (1089–1168) on Kinzan mountain, and would stop over in the priest's quarters. *(Daiye had seven women disciples, and Mujaku was the most beautiful – Imai.)* The head monk Manan always objected strongly. Daiye said to him: 'She is a woman but she has great virtue in her.' Manan still did not approve. Daiye then insisted that he should interview her, and he reluctantly told her that he would come to see her.

When Manan came, Mujaku said: 'Will you make it a dharma-interview, or a worldly interview?'

Manan replied: 'A dharma-interview.'

Mujaku said: 'Then let your attendants depart.' She went in first, and then called to him to enter her room alone. When he came past the curtain he found Mujaku lying face upwards on the bed without anything on at all. He pointed at her and said: 'What is there in here?'

Mujaku replied: 'All the Buddhas of the three worlds and the six patriarchs and the great priests everywhere – they all come out from here.'

Manan said: 'And would you let me enter, or would you not?'

Mujaku replied: 'A donkey might pass: a horse may not pass.'

Manan said nothing, and Mujaku declared: 'The interview with the head monk is ended.' She turned over and showed her back.

Manan turned red and left.

Daiye said, 'The old thing had some insight, didn't she? She outfaced Manan.'

TESTS

(1) Meditate on the spiritual inspiration in Mujaku's dharma-interview, and declare it: Say!

(2) Manan stood silent: find a word to say for him.

This incident became a kōan for the nuns at the interviews of
the nun teacher Shōtaku, a disciple of Daisen, the 17th master
at Enkakuji and who became the third teacher at Tōkeiji.
*(Imai's note: Mujaku and Manan both became well-known in
the Zen world.)*

No. 52.   *The night interview of Nun Myōtei*

*(Imai's note: Myōtei was a widow and a woman well known
for her strength of character. She trained for some years under
Kimon, the 150th Master of Enkakuji; on a chance visit to the
temple she had had an experience while listening to a sermon
by him on the Diamond Sutra. In the year 1568 she took part
in the Rohatsu training week.) (This is the most severe
training week of the year; it is at the beginning of December,
when according to tradition the Buddha meditated six days
and nights, then looked at the morning star and attained full
realization. There is almost continuous meditation broken
only by interviews with the teacher, sūtra chanting, meals and
tea; this goes on for a week, with very little or no sleep
according to the temple. On the morning after the last night's
meditation and interviews the participants look together at
the morning star. – Tr.)*

Before one of the night interviews she took off her robes
and came in without anything on at all. She lay down before
the teacher, who picked up his iron nyo-i (ceremonial stick)
and thrust it out towards her thighs, saying, 'What trick is
this?'

The nun said, 'I present the gate by which all the Buddhas
of the three realms come into the world.'

The teacher said, 'Unless the Buddhas of the three realms go in, they cannot come out. Let the gate be entered here and now' and he sat astride the nun.

She demanded, 'He who should enter, what Buddha is that?'

The teacher said, 'What is to be from the beginning has no "should" about it.'

The nun said, 'He who does not give his name is a barbarian brigand, who is not allowed to enter.'

The teacher said, 'Maitreya Buddha, who has to be born to save the people after the death of Shakyamuni Buddha, enters the gate.'

The nun made as if to speak and the teacher quickly covered her mouth. He pressed the iron stick between her thighs saying, 'Maitreya Buddha enters the gate. Give birth this instant!'

The nun hesitated and the teacher said, 'This is no true womb; how could this give birth to Maitreya?'

The nun went out and at the interview the next morning the teacher said, 'Have you given birth to Maitreya?'

The nun cried with great force, 'He was born quietly last night.' She caught hold of the teacher and put her hands round the top of his head saying, 'I invite the Buddha to take the top of this head as the Lion Throne. Let him graciously preach a sermon from it.'

The teacher said, 'The way is one alone, not two, not three.'

The nun said, 'In their abilities, the beings differ in ten thousand ways. How should you stick to one way?'

The teacher said, 'One general at the head of ten thousand men enters the capital.'

TESTS

(1) What is the real meaning of Myōtei's coming naked for the night interview?

(2) The nun hesitated about giving birth to Maitreya. Say something for her.

(3) What does the one general and the ten thousand soldiers mean? What is it directly? Now say!

This became a kōan in Kamakura Zen, and after the time of the nun Ryōdō, the 7th teacher at Tōkeiji, was given to nuns in the whole eastern part of Japan. *(If this is so, there must be a scribal error in the date at the beginning – Tr.)*

No.'53. The Buddha-heart relics

In the first year of Daiei (1521), Lord Hōjō Ujitsuna built a great temple (the Sōunji at Odawara) at the foot of Mount Hakone, with the idea of wresting religious supremacy from the great temples of the Kantō area (which includes Kamakura). At the time it was widely known that there was a Buddha tooth relic at Enkakuji. Lord Ujitsuna thought he would like to get this and install it in a pagoda built for the purpose, so he sent Fujita Koresada as an envoy to Enkakuji, with the request that the Buddha tooth relic be transferred. Priest Ekihō interviewed him, and told him:

'The Buddha tooth relic is an old treasure of the temple, and I should never dare to move it. But I do have the relic ashes of the Buddha-heart, and if Your Excellency should desire, I can pass them over.'

The envoy went back and told this to the Lord, who somewhat suspiciously told him to ask for them. Tomita accordingly returned to Enkakuji, armed with formal instructions, and on arriving at Enkakuji he asked for the Buddha-heart relics. Ekihō, who was the 153rd master there, saw him, and casually assented. He had tea and cakes served to Tomita, who after drinking the tea said, 'I request that I may be given the ashes now so that I can return at once.'

The priest suddenly shook his whole body and gave a tremendous Katzu! shout, on which the envoy lost consciousness, and did not revive.

The registrar at Enkakuji temple sent a report to Odawara castle saying: 'His Excellency the envoy today was struck by the relics, and died.'

TEST
Right now the envoy is in front of you. Try striking the relics at him. Prove it!
(Imai's note: This is a training in the Katzu! shout.)

This incident became a kōan in Kamakura Zen at the interviews of Keisho, the 153rd master at Enkakuji.

No. 54.   *The Zen Goma rite*

When Zen master Eisai was at Kamakura, he performed the Goma rite for a safe delivery of a child to the wife of Wada Shōgen, and it had a marvellous effect. Accordingly, the latter's grandson, a student of Zen, came on the eighth day of the second month of the first year of Kakei (1387) to Kenchōji, made a reverence to Kyōrin, the 163rd teacher there, and begged him to perform a similar Goma rite for a safe delivery to Fusahimé, his own wife who had been in travail three days and nights of pain.

The teacher said: 'Zen master Eisai was one who came to our Zen originally from the Esoteric schools of Tendai and Shingon, so he was expert in the Goma rite of those sects. But I myself from youth have practised only in Zen training halls, so I never learnt the Shingon ceremonies, and I do not know the Goma rite. Still, in Zen we do have our own way of doing Goma, and if Your Honour thinks that the Zen Goma would be appropriate, I will perform it.'

Wada said: 'My prayer is only that my wife should have a safe delivery, and I have no idea of choosing between the Goma of Zen and the Goma of the Esoteric sect.'

The teacher then called his attendant and told him to light

the stove; he inhaled the smoke, chanting: 'Easy birth, easy birth, very easy birth', and thus performed the rite. It is said that at that very instant Fusahimé gave birth to a boy child, and the contemporaries speak of it as a miracle by the priest.

TESTS

(1) Say what Goma really is.

(2) Leaving Fusahimé's safe delivery for the moment, is the Zen Goma and the Esoteric Goma the same or different? Say!

(3) If 'the same' is not right, and 'different' is not right, then come out and declare what is right.

(4) Suppose someone comes here now and asks you to pray for a safe delivery, what will you do? Say!

(Imai's note: In the Kogetsu school, when Kamakura Zen kōans were given to pupils, they used different means. When the layman Kidō took this kōan with teacher Shunnō (the master at Nanzenji temple) the teacher laid himself down and rubbed his chest and belly as if in labour pains, crying 'Oh what a difficult birth, a difficult birth, such a difficult birth! Get me an easy birth quickly!' and at that time any who hesitated had to taste a blow from his stick.

This kōan seems simple enough but it is one that is passed only with great pains and should not be taken to be easy.)

The incident became a kōan in Kamakura Zen at the interviews of Rinchū, the 171st master at Kenchōji.

No. 55. *The one-word Heart Sūtra*

When Zen Master Daikaku was at the Temple of Great Compassion in Szechuan, having renounced home and become a Buddhist novice, he determined that at the three daily periods of sūtra reading before the images of Buddhas and patriarchs, he would read none of the various sūtras prescribed in the Zen regulations except for the Heart Sūtra, and he said openly:

'The 84,000 scrolls of the Buddha dharma are simply the one scroll of the Heart Sūtra, and that one scroll of 262 words comes down to one word. Reading of many sūtras is like doubting the Buddha.'

The novice bravely followed his own convictions, and calmly read the sūtra of the single scroll.

TESTS

(1) The Heart Sūtra of 262 words: what word do these all come down to?

(2) When the student replies, 'The Heart Sūtra of 262 words (comes down to . . . . . .)' he is asked: 'You said heart; the heart is being born and dying at each thought, and it possesses delusion or realization, and is not unborn, undying, undefiled or impure. Say now, what is it?' (*Imai's note:*)

(3) Then on the point of the Heart Sūtra of one word, 'Buddha' is not it, 'dharma' is not it, 'vision' is not it, 'emptiness' is not it, 'dhāranī-spell' is not it, 'sūtra' is not it. When the student has penetrated to the one word, his insight is in the traditional schools brought under the hammer of eighteen tests.

This incident became a kōan in Kamakura Zen when National Teacher Daiō, the 13th master at Kenchōji, began to use the Heart Sūtra in tests when training Toyama, feudal lord of Tango, and from the time of Kaō, 52nd master at Kenchōji, it began to be used generally in Zen interviews.

No. 56. *Isshin's rain-making*

In the seventh year of Kōan (1284) there was a great drought. In every region the rice-fields and farmlands dried up and there was no sign of anything growing. The Vice-regent (Hōjō Sadatoki) anticipated that such a bad year might cause disturbances in some areas, and he asked the great Zen master Mugaku (Bukkō) to pray for rain according to the traditional ceremony (once) used by Zen master Eisai. He gave orders in the capital that in front of the stone torii of the Tsurugaoka Hachiman shrine at Kamakura an altar twelve foot square should be erected of pure sand, and arrangements made for the ceremony with its accessories of rice-wine and so on.

Bukkō's attendant disciple Isshin (the editor of the Records of Bukkō) did not at all welcome this performance of a rite of the Shingon mantra school, as Eisai, though professing Zen, had done. *(Imai's note: It is said that the rite which Zen Master Eisai performed when he prayed for rain at Kamakura in June 1201 was a ceremony of the Shingon sect with which Eisai had once been connected.)*

Bukkō said to him: 'When you go to a village, follow the village ways. What is wrong with that?'

The attendant, when he saw that the Master was going to do it, hastened away first, and when he got to the altar jumped up on it and said:

'Today instead of the Master let this novice make the prayer for rain. The Zen way of rain-making is an unusual one. Do Your Honours please look,' and he briskly tucked up his robe, spread his legs wide, stuck out the 'one-eyed dragon' and made water on the altar.

At this Sasaki Sukemori, the official in charge of the ceremony, was aghast and angry. He arrested the disciple and was taking him under escort to the Kita-mandokoro police headquarters, when on the way suddenly a great downpour fell, bathing the road. Sasaki realized that there had been a divine meaning in Isshin's action of making water, formally thanked him with warmth and set him free.

TESTS
(1) Where is the rain-god? Say!

(2) What virtue was there in Isshin's action? Say!

(3) If there is virtue in making water on an altar, then this instant try making water on this Buddha-altar to test the virtue. Make the proof of it!

(4) The teacher lifts his nyo-i stick and says, 'This thing, and Isshin's one-eyed dragon – are they really in the end the same or different? Say!'

(5) If you really understand, try manifesting great action immediately: make proof of it!

(Imai's note: Many koji (laymen) taking this test have tried imitating the action of making water, and received a slap on the face from the teacher for it. Don't imitate them!)

This became a kōan in Kamakura Zen at the interviews of Kōan, the 14th teacher at Enkakuji.

No. 57. Bukkō's death poem

On the first day of the ninth month of the ninth year of Kōan (1286) Bukkō, Teacher of the Nation (Kokushi), developed symptoms of illness which he realized he would not survive. He wrote a note to the Government officials and old friends to tell them that he would take his departure on the third day of that month.

Just at dawn on the third day he wrote a poem for them:

> Buddhas and ordinary men are equally illusions.
> If you go looking for the true form, it is a speck of dust in the eye.
> The burnt bones of this old monk embrace heaven and earth;
> Do not scatter the cold ashes to mountain and sky.

That night at the third watch he changed his robe and, sitting in the meditation posture, took up a brush and wrote:

114

Coming, and no more going on:
Going, and no more returning.
With a mane of a million hairs, that lion appears:
With its mane of a million hairs, the lion roars.

TESTS

(1) Bukkō announced the moment of his death three days before. Now without any promptings, do you declare the time of your own departure. Say!

(Imai's note: In this first question, the word 'departure' has to be understood in its Zen sense.)

(2) The Teacher of the Nation said: 'Buddhas and ordinary men are equally illusions.' Now say: Is there someone who is not illusion, or is there not?

(3) Right now who is the one who makes the duality of the illusions? Say!

(4) The Teacher said, 'The burnt bones of this old monk embrace heaven and earth.' Now say: Who is this who embraces the old monk's bones? Speak!

(5) The Teacher said: 'With its mane of a million hairs, that lion appears, and roars.' Now say: Where is this lion roaring right now?

This became a kōan at the interviews of Daien, the 3rd master at Enkakuji.

No. 58.   The charm

In the Jōwa era (1345–9) the Kamakura region was in great terror from raids of brigands in the aftermath of the civil war. At the request of the country people, some of the temples began to produce amulets, charms against robbers, for distribution to their followers.

But the Zen temples, which have never recommended such

things, refused to follow the lead of the other temples, and did not give out any amulets.

At the time, the Jizō at Saida was talked of far and wide for its spiritual power in warding off danger, and many people came to the temple to pray before it.

So Yuiheita Tomochika, a country samurai of Koshigoe, and a follower of Zen, during a visit to the Buddha hall had an audience with priest Kakkai, to make a request. He explained the general fear of robbers, and begged again and again that the priest would follow those of other temples, and give him an amulet charm. Then Kakkai at once took up a brush and wrote a single character on a piece of paper, sealed it, and gave it to him as a charm.

Yuiheita reverently put it to his head. Then, it is said, for two nights he meditated till he penetrated into it, and so became completely free of fear.

TESTS

(1) What could be the virtue of a single character as a charm?
(2) What was that one character on which Yuiheita meditated and became free of fear?

This became a kōan at the interviews of Daisetsu, the 69th master at Kenchōji.

No. 59. *Ashikaga Takauji's Jizō-Son*

(Translator's note: This story depends on a sort of play on a Chinese character of twelve strokes, which means 'honoured' or 'revered'. It is the first element of the name Taka-uji, the general who founded the Ashikaga shōgunate, after a spectacular betrayal of trust of a kind not uncommon in Japanese mediaeval history. The same character is added to the name of Jizō, bodhisattva of protection, in which case it is read 'Son', and not 'Taka'. It is similarly added to the word

for *'protective charm'* (*mamori*). *In order to retain the effect of the story, I am rendering the Ashikaga general's name as Ashikaga-Son, to keep the assonance with Jizō-Son.*)

At Jōmyōji temple in Kamakura, there was a picture of Jizō-son by the brush of Ashikaga-Son himself. General Ashikaga Mochiuji (of the same family, later governor of the Eastern Provinces) wanted to have this as a protective charm (mamori-Son) with his armour, and asked priest Daizui whether he could have the loan of it.

The priest said loudly: 'General!'

'Yes?' he replied.

'Who is it that has just said Yes? Jizō-Son is there, and must not go seeking from others.' The nobleman understood.

TESTS

(1) Priest Mitsudō of Hōkokuji temple tested the samurai Ōta with the questions:
Where does Jizō-Son go back to?
What was it that the general understood?

(2) Mitsudō tested Masuda Moto-o: When Ashikaga-Son paints Jizō-Son, does Ashikaga become Jizō, or Jizō become Ashikaga? Say!

(3) He tested general Hosokawa:
When they hold up the picture of Jizō-Son by the brush of Ashikaga-Son himself, if you name it Jizō, well, it is Ashikaga; and if you name it Ashikaga, why it·is Jizō. Then what will you do to give this a name? Say!

(4) He tested Gendazaemon Michinaga:
The governor of the Eastern Provinces, in the 23rd year of Ōei (1416), asked to borrow the Jizō-Son painted by Ashikaga-Son himself, to have as a charm-Son in his camp. Now say, what result is there from having Jizō-Son in the camp?

This became a Kamakura Zen kōan at the interviews of

Mitsudō (who was abbot at both Jōmyōji and Hōkokuji temples).

No. 60. *The gravestone with no name*

The gravestone of the priest who founded Hōkokuji, by his final instructions, records no name. There is just a great stone on top of the grave to mark the place. Thereafter many of the chief priests of Hōkokuji followed this precedent of the founder, and there are many graves without any name on them.

Uesugi Shigemitsu, a student of Zen, once came to Hōkokuji and paid his respects to Hakudō, the 5th master there. He said:

'At this temple there are gravestones with no name. It will mean that future generations will hardly be able to tell whose graves they are.'

The priest said: 'After they are dead, what would the line of priests of this temple want with names? Have you not heard that it is said: "The four great rivers enter the ocean and lose their name"?'

The nobleman said: 'But with the years, the ground may change, and if they do not know the graves, their successors in the dharma will find it impossible to perform the usual worship at the graves of their predecessors.'

The Master said: 'The spiritual gravestones of the line of priests of this temple are in the very depths of the heart of their successors in the dharma. If there is not in Your Honour's own heart the spiritual gravestone of your illustrious ancestor, then worship before even a towering five-storied pagoda will be meaningless.'

The noble said: 'Your Reverence is the chief priest of this temple of which my illustrious ancester laid the foundation. Is then the spiritual gravestone of my ancestor in Your Reverence's heart?'

Before he could finish, the priest seized him and threw him down under the pinetree among the graves, and said: 'Look, look! Here is the spiritual gravestone, here it is!' The noble grasped a meaning behind the words and said:

'From the very depths of the gravestone without a name come the founder of the temple and the layer of the foundation, holding hands, clear before us!'

TESTS

(1) Hakudō said: 'The spiritual gravestones of the line of priests of this temple are in the very depths of the heart of their successors in the dharma.' Now say: the line of gravestones in the depths of the heart, how do you perform the rite before them, how do you worship them?

(2) How do the founder of the temple and the layer of the foundation join hands and come before you together? Say!

This incident became a kōan in Kamakura Zen at the interviews of Mitsudō, master of Hōkokuji temple.

No. 61. *The judgment of Yama*

The shrine of Yama (judge of the dead) on Mt Mikoshi at Yui in Kamakura was transferred by Lord Ashikaga Takauji to Arai, where it was installed with a consecration ceremony. On that occasion Nobuchika, a student of Zen, entered the shrine and asked the priest in charge:

'King Yama, we are told, is in hell where he passes judgment on the sinners from this world. But what Buddha is it who passes judgment on the sin of King Yama?'

The priest had no words.

TESTS

(1) Bring a word for the priest.

119

(2) What sin would there be in Yama? Say!

This incident became a kōan in Kamakura Zen in the interviews of priest Sōden, namely Zen master Chikaku of Enkakuji.

No. 62.   *Really before the eyes*

Realizing he was about to die, Priest Nanshū, on the twenty-first day of the first month of the first year of Kagen (1303) made his death poem in the verse:

> T'ang (China) and Japan,
>> Sixty-three years;
> If you want to know it,
>> See what is before your eyes.

TEST
What does this Before Your Eyes really mean?

This death poem became a kōan at the interviews of Donpū, the 45th Master at Enkakuji.
(Imai's note: Nanshū's real name was Kōkai, and his posthumous name was Zen Master Shinnō; he was the successor to Gottan and founded the subtemple Zōunan at Jōchiji. When he was there he used to handle Zen inquirers without giving any classical kōan at all, and he would test the warrior pupils with the words: If you want to know it, See what is before your eyes. This appears as the second half of his death poem also.

In the Sōringakki account it is entitled the Kōan Of Before The Eyes, but in this Shōnankattōroku it is given as Really Before The Eyes.)

No. 63.   So

In the first year of Tokuji (1306), on the eighteenth day of the fifth month, Priest Mushō, aware of impending death, shouted a Katzu! and cried:

> All the Buddhas come *so*,
> All the Buddhas go *so;*
> How all the Buddhas come and go
> Now I teach: *So.*

TEST
What does *so* mean?

(Imai's note: His posthumous name was Hōkai. He went to Sung China, where he received the dharma from Master Sekkai, and on returning founded a subtemple at Jōchiji. When he was at Jōchiji he patiently received Zen inquirers, but if they asked directly about Zen he used to reply with the one word: So, and resolutely refused to engage in wordy Zen. His death poem presents the word So and this collection of Kamakura kōans heads this one with the title So.)

No. 64.   The picture of beauty

In 1299 when Fukada Sadatomo came to Kenchōji for a ceremony, he met the teacher in a room where there happened to be a picture of the contemporary Sung dynasty beauty Rei Shōjo. He asked Master Saikan, 'Who is that?'

The teacher replied, 'It is said it happens to be Rei Shōjo.'

Sadatomo looked at the picture admiringly and remarked, 'That picture is powerfully painted and yet of the utmost delicacy. Is that woman now in the Sung country (China)?'

The teacher said, 'What do you mean, in the Sung? Now, here, in Japan.'

The noble said, 'And where is that?'

The master said loudly, 'Lord Sadatomo!'
The noble looked up.
'And where is that?' said the teacher.
Sadatomo grasped the point and bowed.

TEST
What did Lord Sadatomo grasp?

This became a kōan at Kenchōji from the time of Dōan, the
105th master there.

No. 65. *How the sūtra of the Resolution of the Brahma-king's Doubt was put into the canon*

Atsushige, a warrior who was a student of the Shingon
(mantra) sect, came to Jōraku temple and asked priest Jikusen
about the kōans made from scriptures in the so-called nyōrai
Zen or Buddha Zen. The teacher said:

'They are of many kinds. One of them is this: When the
Buddha had just been born, he said, "Above heaven or under
heaven, I alone am the world-honoured one." Then when he
completed the path, he declared: "Wonderful! All beings have
innately the nature of the wisdom of the Buddha."

'Then, before his entry into Nirvāṇa, there was an incident
when he held up a flower in his fingers, and there was a smile
(from Mahākāśyapa alone of the spectators). In this last case,
the meaning of Zen was being presented without any
involvement with words at all.'

The warrior said: 'The incident of the smile comes in the
sūtra called The Resolution of the Brahma-king's Doubt. But
that is not in the canon of authentic scriptures. Probably it
was made up by some Zen man of the T'ang dynasty.'

The teacher cried, 'Atsushige!'

'Yes?' he replied.

'Who has made up this Yes?' said the teacher.

Atsushige made a bow and went out. After three days he had a realization. He came back and said to the teacher: 'The sūtra of the Resolution of the Brahma-king's Doubt has at last been put in the canon.'

TESTS

(1) Who is this Brahma-king? Say!
(2) How was the Brahma-king's doubt really resolved? Say!
(3) What is this putting of the Brahma-king's doubt into the canon?

This became a kōan at the interviews of master Ryōdō (Zen master Honkaku, the 35th teacher at Kenchōji).

No. 66. *The mark of the Brahma-voice*

Unjōbō, maker of Buddha images who was always regarded as second only to the famous master Unkei, worked at Kamakura where his pieces were much esteemed. Accordingly Priest Rinsō, namely Zen Master Kakushō of Jufukuji, ordered Unjōbō to make a Buddha image for a memorial service for those who had fallen in the war of Genkō (1331). He carved a wooden image modelled on the main Buddha of Jufukuji. Full of pride in his skill, he remarked as he presented it, that the image faithfully embodied all thirty-two of the traditional marks of the Buddha.

The teacher said: 'Of the thirty-two marks, the twenty-eighth is the Brahma-voice, deep and far-reaching. Does this carving of yours show that?'

Unjōbō pondered silently for a long time, but could find no answer.

He confined himself in the Buddha hall of Jufukuji for twenty-one days, praying for light on the Brahma-voice mark of a Buddha. On the last day of the vow he had a realization, went to the teacher's interview room and said:

(What Unjōbō said has to be supplied by the pupil)

TESTS

(1) From among the thirty-two marks, how is the Brahma-voice mark to be made by the sculptor? – Say!

(2) What did Unjōbō say to the teacher? Speak!

This became a kōan in Kamakura Zen at the interviews of Katsugan, the 126th master at Kenchōji.

No. 67. *The mind, the Buddha; no mind, no Buddha*

Kenyū, a teacher of the Ritsu (Vinaya) sect, once visited Jufukuji, and when he met Jakuan, namely Zen Master Kōkō, he asked:

'I have heard that in your Zen there is a saying: *The mind, the Buddha; no mind, no Buddha.* What does it mean?'

The teacher said: 'Let the Ajari (teacher) find the right two phrases in the Heart Sūtra, and he will grasp the meaning.'

TESTS

(1) What are the two phrases in the Heart Sūtra?

(2) When you have these phrases, how do you grasp the meaning of *The mind, the Buddha; no mind, no Buddha*? Say!

This became a kōan at the interviews of priest Chūei, the 110th master at Enkakuji.

No. 68. *The Great Katzu! of Master Tōden*

Yoriyasu was a swaggering and aggressive samurai. *(Imai's note: In the Nirayama manuscript of Bukedōshinshū and in some other accounts the name is given as Yorihara.)* In the spring of 1341 he was transferred from Kōfu to Kamakura,

124

where he visited Master Tōden, the 45th teacher at Kenchōji, to ask about Zen.

The teacher said, 'It is to manifest directly the Great Action in the hundred concerns of life. When it is loyalty as a samurai, it is the loyalty of Zen. "Loyalty" is written with the Chinese character made up of "centre" and "heart", so it means the lord in the centre of the man. There must be no wrong passions. But when this old priest looks at the samurai today, there are some whose heart centre leans towards name and money, and others where it is towards wine and lust, and with others it is inclined towards power and bravado. They are all on those slopes, and cannot have a centred heart; how could they have loyalty to the state? If you, Sir, wish to practise Zen, first of all practise loyalty and do not slip into wrong desires.'

The warrior said, 'Our loyalty is direct Great Action on the battlefield. What need have we for sermons from a priest?'

The teacher replied, 'You, Sir, are a hero in strife, I am a gentleman of peace – we can have nothing to say to each other.'

The warrior then drew his sword and said, 'Loyalty is in the hero's sword, and if you do not know *this*, you should not talk of loyalty.'

The teacher replied, 'This old priest has the treasure sword of the Diamond King, and if you do not know it, you should not talk of the source of loyalty.'

The samurai said, 'Loyalty of your Diamond Sword – what is the use of that sort of thing in actual fighting?'

The teacher jumped forward and gave one Katzu! shout, giving the samurai such a shock that he lost consciousness. After some time the teacher shouted again and the samurai at once recovered. The teacher said, 'The loyalty in the hero's sword, where is it? Speak!'

The samurai was over-awed; he apologized and took his departure.

(Imai's note: In the account in the sixth volume of Gosan-

125

nyūdōshū it is added that Yorihara wept and presented his sword in token of repentance.)

TEST

Right now before you is that samurai. Try a shout that the teacher may see the proof.

This became a kōan in Kamakura Zen from the time of Koten, the 57th teacher at Kenchōji.

Variation No. 68. The Great Katzu! of Master Tōrin

The Tōkeiji nunnery at Kamakura was known as the Divorce Temple, because if a woman of the samurai class who was unhappy in marriage entered there and stayed three years, the marriage link was dissolved, by an Imperial rescript given by Emperor Gofukakusa at the request of the Hōjō regent Sadatoki. Later a period of one year's residence was made sufficient, by a ruling of the Ashikaga Government for the temple regulations.

In the third year of Enbun (1358), Ashikaga Motouji sent a man to decoy Nitta Yoshioki to Yakuchiwatashi in Musashi, and kill him there. Motouji's wife Akijo, herself born into the Nitta clan, was overwhelmed with grief at the treacherous murder of Yoshioki, and requested to be allowed to become a nun to pray for his soul. But this was not acceded to.

Apprehending that there might now be some danger to herself also, she made a hurried escape from the palace and hid herself in Tōkeiji. When she had been there a year, Kanemitsu, a minister of the Governor, came to know of it, and arrived determined to take her away by force. The nun Ekō, who had the position of shitsuji at Tōkeiji, at once sent across to Enkakuji to ask the Abbot to come. This was Tōrin, the 32nd master there, and when he came he greeted

Kanemitsu, and explained the regulations for the temple under which it would be forbidden to arrest Akijo, who would have right of sanctuary. Kanemitsu became angry and drew his sword to threaten the Abbot with it. The latter remonstrated with him against the use of violence but he refused to listen.

Tōrin on the instant gave a great Katsu! shout, and Kanemitsu fell unconscious. After a little, the Abbot shouted again and Kanemitsu revived. The teacher then said: 'The rule that after three years here, the marriage bond is severed was laid down in an Imperial rescript of the Emperor Gofukakusa, and the regulation that even one year would be sufficient was an ordinance of General Ashikaga Takauji. These decrees have never been broken, and for a minister of the Governor here to violate the sanctuary would be no light offence.' As he continued speaking, Kanemitsu found himself unable to reply; he fell into a convulsion and died.

TEST

Right now before you is a ruffian with drawn sword threatening your life. Try whether you can kill and revive him with a Katsu! Show the proof.

This became a kōan in Kamakura Zen at the interviews of Chintei, the 47th master at Enkakuji.
(Imai's note: Those two kōans involving a Katsu! to kill and revive were very difficult to pass. There are other kōans in the Shōnankattōroku where a Katsu! is used to strike down, but there are only three where this is to be followed by a second Katsu! to bring back to consciousness. In the commentary to the Sōrinzakki, No. 68 and its variant are called The Great Barrier of The Two Tō's (i.e. Tōden and Tōrin).

At the time when Kamakura Zen flourished, there had to be a teacher who could demonstrate in actual practice in this way in order to handle the warrior students of

Zen. To pass this kōan the pupil had to apply the striking and reviving Katzu! shouts to some bird or dog and so on outside the interview room. These days when Zen is enfeebled, there is not one in a hundred who could do so. It is said that Yamaoka Tesshū took these tests under the hammer of Master Genō of Chōtokuji, and later perfected them under Master Ryūtaku. Katsu Kaishū, again, took them at Kotokuji under Master Kisatei, and is reported to have had a hard time with them. But since the Meiji Restoration we hardly hear of any who have done so, which bespeaks weakness of samādhi power and an enfeeblement of Zen.)

No. 69.   The paper sword

In 1331 when Nitta Yoshisada was fighting against Hōjō Sadatoki, a chief retainer of the Hōjō family, named Sakurada Sadakuni, was slain. His wife Sawa wished to pray for the dead man; she cut off her hair and entered Tōkeiji as the nun Shōtaku. For many years she devoted herself to Zen under Daisen, the 17th master at Enkakuji, and in the end she became the 3rd teacher of Tōkeiji. In the Rōhatsu training week of December 1338 she was returning from her evening interview with the teacher at Enkakuji, when on the way a man armed with a sword saw her and was attracted by her beauty. He threatened her with the sword and came to rape her. The nun took out a piece of paper and rolled it up, then thrust it like a sword at the man's eyes. He became unable to strike and was completely overawed by her spiritual strength. He turned to run and the nun gave a Katsu! shout, hitting him with the paper sword. He fell and then fled.

TEST

Show the paper sword which is the heart sword, and prove its actual effect now.

(Imai's note: The manifestation of the paper sword as a real sword is from the cultivation of the Kikai Tanden (the elixir field in the energy sea — see No. 92), and originally in Kamakura Zen all the teachers gave this test. Ōishi Yoshina (of the 47 Rōnin) took this kōan under Master Bankei, and Araki Matauemon under Takuan at Nanshūji — so it is reported in Shōsō Manpitsu, vol. 7.

When Araki encountered Yagyu Tajimanokami, the latter was teacher of fencing to the Shōgun, and it was the rule that any samurai who wished to meet him had to leave behind both swords in the waiting room. Informed of this, Araki took off his weapons. When he came before Yagyu, the latter wished to test his spirit, and suddenly challenged him to a duel, drawing his own weapon. According to the old accounts, Araki snatched up a piece of paper, rolled it up and was able to meet Yagyu with it as a sword. There is a widespread tradition in the Zen world about this contest, and it is accepted that Araki was able to manifest the paper as a sword by virtue of having taken this Kamakura kōan of the paper sword under Master Takuan in his interview room.)*

No. 70.   Heaven and earth broken up

Tadamasa, a senior retainer of Hōjō Takatoki the Regent, had the Buddhist name Anzan (quiet mountain). He was a keen Zen follower and for twenty-three years came and went to the meditation hall for laymen at Kenchōji. When the fighting broke out everywhere in 1331, he was wounded in one engagement, but in spite of the pain galloped to Kenchōji to see Sozan, the 27th teacher there. A tea ceremony was going on at Kenchōji, and the teacher seeing the man in armour come in, quickly put a teacup in front of him and said, 'How is this?'

The warrior at once crushed it under his foot and said, 'Heaven and earth broken up altogether.'

The teacher said, 'When heaven and earth are broken up, how is it with you?'

Anzan stood with his hands crossed over his breast. The teacher hit him, and he involuntarily cried out from the pain of his wounds.

The teacher said, 'Heaven and earth not quite broken up yet.'

The drum sounded from the camp across the mountain, and Tadamasa galloped quickly back. The next evening he came again, covered with blood, to see the teacher. The teacher came out and said again,

'When heaven and earth are broken up, how it is with you?'

Anzan, supporting himself on his blood-stained sword, gave a great Katzu! and died standing in front of the teacher.

TEST
When heaven and earth are broken up, how is it with you?
(Imai's note: In the Bukedōshinshū, the version is: When the elements of the body are dispersed, where are you?)

This began to be used as a kōan in the interviews of priest Jikusen, the 29th master of Kenchōji.

No. 71.   *Victory in the midst of a hundred enemies*

To priest Yōzan, the 28th teacher at Enkakuji, came for an interview a samurai named Ryōzan, who practised Zen. The teacher said:

'You are going into the bath-tub, stark naked without a stitch on. Now a hundred enemies in armour, with bows and swords, appear all around you. How will you meet them? Will you crawl before them and beg for mercy? Will you show your warrior birth by dying in combat against them? or does a man of the Way get some special holy grace?'

Ryōzan said, 'Let me win without surrendering and without fighting.'

TEST

Caught in the midst of the hundred enemies, how will you manage to win without surrendering and without fighting?

(Imai's note: This first became a kōan at the interviews of Tōryō, founder of the Tō-un-an temple at Enkakuji. Later in Tokugawa times, Suzuki Shōzan used it to put his samurai pupils under the hammer.)

No. 72.   *Teaching Buddhism*

One day Nobuchika came to Jufukuji at Kamakura to have an interview with Butchi Ennō, known as Kengai. Nobuchika said:

'Tenryū teaches Buddhism by a single finger. But this old warrior on the battlefield, even if he lost both his arms, can teach Buddhism by one leg', and saying this, he lifted up his right leg.

The teacher seized it and pushed it away, saying:

'And when you have no leg, what will you use to teach Buddhism with?'

The warrior lifted his eyebrows and blinked his eyes.

The teacher said: 'And when you lose your eyes, what then?'

Nobuchika made to open his mouth, but the teacher seized him and covered his mouth, saying, 'When you lose your mouth, then what?'

The old warrior could not make a reply.

TEST
Preach Buddhism for this warrior.

This incident became a theme in the interviews of Gassan who was the founder of the Keiinan sub-temple at Jufukuji.

No. 73. *Pasting the charm on the heart*

The hall of Yakushi (the Buddha of healing) at Shōganan temple at the pagoda of Hōkokuji in Kamakura became widely renowned for its spiritual virtue against plague. After the fighting in the Genkō era (1331), there was a succession of epidemics, and Yamanouchi Sadahira asked at the temple for a paper charm against sickness, adding:

'I have heard that the charm has to be pasted up on the gate pillar of one's house. But my own house has been completely burnt during the fighting, and now I have nowhere to live; I am camping under the trees in the valley, and have no gate pillar. So how and where can I stick this up?'

Daikyō, the priest of Shōganan, said:

'Stick it on your heart.'

TEST

The heart has no form: how can a charm be stuck on to it?

This came to be used as a kōan in Kamakura Zen when Daikyō began to give it to test all the Zen students who came to practise zazen meditation in the Yakushi hall.

No. 74. *Painting the nature*

Ekichū, the 7th master of Jufukuji, was famous as a painter. One day Nobumitsu came to see him and asked whether he could paint the fragrance described in the famous line 'After walking through flowers, the horse's hoof is fragrant.' The teacher drew a horse's hoof and a butterfly fluttering round it (attracted by the fragrance).

Then Nobumitsu quoted the line 'Spring breeze over the river bank' and asked for a picture of the breeze. The teacher drew a branch of willow waving.

Nobumitsu cited the famous Zen phrase, 'A finger direct to the human heart, See the nature to be Buddha.' He asked for a picture of the heart. The teacher picked up the brush and flicked a spot of ink onto Nobumitsu's face. The warrior was surprised and annoyed, and the teacher rapidly sketched the angry face.

Then Nobumitsu asked for a picture of the 'nature' as in the phrase 'see the nature'. The teacher broke the brush and said, 'That's the picture.'

Nobumitsu did not understand and the teacher remarked, 'If you haven't got that seeing eye, you can't see it.'

Nobumitsu said, 'Take another brush and paint the picture of the nature.'

The teacher replied: 'Show me your nature and I will paint it.'

Nobumitsu had no words.

TESTS

(1) How would you show the nature?
(2) Come, see your nature and bring the proof of it.
(3) Say something for Nobumitsu.

This incident became a kōan in Kamakura Zen at the interviews of Mitsudō of Hōkokuji.

No. 75. *Not going, not coming*

One night of the Rōhatsu training week, in the third year of Jōwa (1347) at Kenchōji, a senior priest Dōshū went to a cave for a night-sitting meditation, and came back at the third watch (about midnight). The monk who was guarding the door of the meditation hall scolded him, saying:

'Where have you been all this time?'
He replied in a sūtra verse:

> Not going, not coming, the primal deep –
> Neither in nor out nor in the middle.

The monk on guard said: 'This sūtra-copier has got both
his eyes; I suppose I ought to let him come in again.'
*(Imai's note: It was known that Dōshū had once copied out
the 25th chapter of the Lotus sūtra in his own blood.)*

TESTS

(1) What does *Not going, not coming,* really mean?
(2) If it is not inside nor outside nor in the middle, where is it?

This incident became a kōan in Kamakura Zen at the
interviews of Jitsuō, the 36th master at Kenchōji.

No. 76.   *The way of the teacup*

In the spring of the first year of Ryakuō (1338), the Imperial
tutor Lord Tadanori came from Kyōto to Kamakura to teach
the Confucian doctrines to the warriors of the Government
there. By the Jōwa era (1345) there were over 360 who were
studying under him, among them the Jōmyōji temple librarian
Tachibana, who showed great talent for study. Zen master
Tentaku, the 41st master at Enkakuji, admonished him,
saying: 'You have talent for scholarship but no bent for Zen.
Perhaps you will not be able to pursue the holy Path. The
Confucian scholars say that the Way has its basis in heaven,
but cannot speak of the Way before heaven and earth were
separated out. If you want to know the true source of the
Way, you must sit in meditation on the mat in the meditation
hall till the perspiration runs from your whole body.'
The librarian reported this to Lord Tadanori, who was

angry and went to Enkakuji to see the teacher. He asked him about the Way, to which the Master replied:

'Confucius says that if one hears the Way in the morning, one can die in the evening content. This is the Way which is the basis of the whole universe. How does your Honour explain it?'

The nobleman opened his mouth to take the floor, when the teacher waved his hand and said: 'The source of the Way is before the three powers (heaven, earth and man) exist: how can Your Honour explain it by mouth and tongue?'

The Imperial tutor retorted: 'Then how would a priest point out the Way?'

The master at once put a cup of fresh tea before him, and said:

'Do you understand?'

The nobleman was at a loss, and the teacher said: 'My Lord, you have not yet the talent for knowing the Way.'

TEST
How is the Way in a cup of tea? Say!

This became a kōan in Kamakura Zen at the interviews of Shunoku, the 54th master at Enkakuji.
(Imai's note: This kōan resembles Jōshū's 'Have a cup of tea', but the meaning is not the same. One has to penetrate into the real meaning of serving tea.)

No. 77. *The scriptures of one hand*

When Enkakuji temple was destroyed by fire in the seventh year of Ōan (1374), the sūtra repository and the library were both completely consumed, and the Buddhist and Confucian texts which Bukkō the founder had brought from China were reduced to ashes. Priests of the Hachiman shrine came to

Enkakuji, concerned about the tragic loss of these T'ang and Sung dynasty texts.

Fumon, the 33rd master at Enkakuji, said to them:

'None of the texts have been burnt.'

'Then where are they?' asked a priest doubtfully.

The teacher drew a circle, and said, 'They are in here.'

The priests did not understand, and one of them said: 'Would you show us the T'ang edition of the Mahā-vairocana sūtra?'

The Master held up one hand. The priests did not know what to make of it.

Another of them asked: 'Will you show us the later translations of the Lotus sūtra (i.e. not by Kumārajīva)?' The Master held up one hand.

A priest asked: 'Please show us the translation of the Sūtra of the Brahma King's Doubt.' The teacher again held up one hand.

A Confucian scholar asked to see a copy of the Zen comments by the poet Sotōba (Su T'ung Po) and the Four Confucian Classics, and the Master again held up one hand.

Then the Ajari (teacher of the Shingon sect) Kōjō said: 'We came here concerned that the T'ang and Sung texts had been lost in the fire, but Your Reverence told us that they were not lost. But when some of us asked to see them, you held up your right hand. What is this supposed to mean?'

The Master said: 'The covers got burnt, but the texts themselves are things to be grasped in the hand. I tried to show this – to those with eyes to see.'

TESTS

(1) What is the real meaning of Fumon's holding up his hand?

(2) Grasp 10,000 scrolls in the hand: bring the proof of it!

This incident became a kōan in Kamakura Zen at the interviews of Donpū, the 45th master at Enkakuji.

No. 78. *Daibai's shari-pearls*

Sakuma Suketake of Ōkura (in the Kamakura region), a student of Zen, was known in the world as Demon Sakuma. For many years he was in active service in the army, but finally his left hand and right leg were disabled by wounds so that he could no longer take part in warfare. He entered the monks' training hall at Enkakuji and practised hard at Zen for over ten years, being given the name Lay brother Daibai. In the winter of the first year of Ōei (1394) there was a great snowfall during the Rōhatsu week, and following the precedent of Tanka's Buddha-burning *(see No. 94 – Tr.)*, he found in the Jizō hall outside the mountain gate a Buddha-image whose wood was rotting away, and was setting light to it against the freezing cold when the lay brother in charge of the Hōunkaku hall at the mountain gate shouted at him to stop.

Daibai said: 'What is wrong with burning a wooden Buddha whose ashes will have no shari-pearls?'

The other was a huge man of great strength, and he pushed Daibai towards the fire saying: '*Your* ashes certainly will have no shari-pearls, so let us burn you.'

Daibai shouted in a fury: 'How would you know whether my ashes have pearls or not? If you want to know about my ashes, I will show you!' and he jumped into the now blazing fire, gave a great Katzu! shout and died standing. His body was consumed, and when the fire had died out, there were eight shari-pearls shining there.

TESTS

(1) The test says: Have your ashes shari-pearls? Say how many, and bring the proof.

(2) Putting aside for the moment dying in the fire, die standing here and now on the tatami mats, and bring the proof!

This incident became a kōan in the interviews of Donbō, the 58th master of Enkakuji and the 59th at Kenchōji.

(Imai's note: In much later times there were cases where a live charcoal was put into the pupil's hand at the interview, and to pass this kōan he had to remain calm, to make the demonstration of Daibai's dying standing in the fire. But this kind of thing is a degeneration of Zen. It cannot compare with the traditional Zen, where the pupil standing before the teacher gave one Katzu! and passed into samādhi. The kōan cannot be passed without a keen Zen spirit and practice of some years.)

No. 79. *The lotus strainer*

Yasunaga, a government official and a student of Zen, came to the Dragon Flower of the Golden Peak (the Shinsaiin hall in Jōchiji temple) to pay his respects to priest Mushō there.

He told him: 'These days the followers of Nichiren are saying that in the present degenerate Latter Days, the water of the dharma in the Buddha ocean has become polluted. It is so contaminated that the impurity must be strained off before it is drunk. The only pure water is what has been purified by being strained through the Lotus sūtra, and this is the dharma taught by Nichiren. Is what they are saying right?'

The priest said: 'Strain off the lotus.'

TESTS
(1) How would you strain off the lotus?
(2) When you have strained and drunk, say how you find it: cold or hot?

This incident became a kōan in Kamakura Zen at the interviews of Tōin, the 10th master at Zenkōji.

No. 80. *The copy*

The head monk of Daitetsudō training temple came to

Gyokuzan, the 21st master at Kenchōji, and saluted him. He then asked whether he might copy out the sermons on the Rinzairoku which had been given by Daikaku, the founder of Kenchōji.

The teacher sat silent for a good time, and then said: 'Have you copied it?'

'Why,' said the head monk, 'I have not yet had the loan of it.'

The teacher replied: 'Rinzai's Zen is communicated from heart to heart – what should you want with writing? If you feel you want to have something in writing, take Mount Ashigara as the brush and Yui shore as the inkstone, and make your copy.'

The head monk gave a Katzu! shout and said: 'I have made my copy.'

TESTS

(1) How can the writing of the founder be copied by a shout?
(2) Try a Katzu! yourself and make proof of it.

This incident became a kōan in Kamakura Zen with the interviews of Kosen, the 38th master at Kenchōji.

No. 81.   *The gate-keeper's question*

In the fighting of the Genkō era (from 1331), there were 2,600 warriors of the Nitta forces encamped at Kobukuro (near Kenchōji), brave men resolved to die in battle. Endō Takahiro, a student of Zen, had the most impressive reputation among them all. One day of strong winds and driving rain, he thought of transferring their camp to Kenchōji, and went to tell the temple. As he was going to enter the gate, the gate-keeper, the priest Shōgai Zenkan, stopped him and asked: 'What is your business?'

He said: 'What I have to say is for the chief priest.'

The gate-keeper said: 'First explain to the gate-keeper what your business is.' *(There were many violent men among the warriors during the war, and the temple rule was that an inquirer must first be examined by the gate-keeper before he could see the chief priest – Imai.)*

Endō, angered, drew his sword and threatened him with it, saying,

'I wanted to ask the chief priest about the Buddhism of the naked sword. Can you say something for him?'

Zenkan gave a Katzu! shout, and wrested the sword from him. Saying, 'The Diamond Treasure Sword belongs in the square inch (of the heart)', he put it away in his long sleeve.

The warrior said: 'When it comes out of the square inch, how is it then?'

The gate-keeper spread all his fingers and danced. Endō was at a loss. The gate-keeper joined his palms in reverent salutation, then again spread out his fingers in front of Endō's face, and danced.

This time he had a realization, made a salutation in gratitude, and went back. Seeing him returning to their camp, Kawada Kakeyoshi asked him, 'What about our moving camp to Kenchōji?'

Endō said: 'We are warriors resolved to die, and even if thunderbolts fall from the sky, we shall not run away. Are we going to become such cowards that we run away to the priests' place from a bit of wind and rain?'

Thus Kenchōji, was spared becoming a war base.

TESTS

(1) What was the real meaning of what the gate-keeper did?
(2) What did that heroic warrior realize, that he bowed in gratitude?

This incident became a kōan in Kamakura Zen at the interviews of Ketsuō, the 50th master at Kenchōji.

140

No. 82.   *The Buddha's birthday*

For the ceremony of the Buddha's birthday, there was a little pavilion near Tōkeiji which had belonged to the Hōjō family from ancient times. *(The nun temple at Tōkeiji was and is famous for the beautiful flowers by the lake, especially azaleas, which can be viewed from the slope above the temple. – Tr.)* These flowers were in full splendour on the Birthday of April 8 each year, and many of those who came to the Kamakura temples to worship on that day used to come to admire the flowers at Tōkeiji. On that April day in the tenth year of Kōan (1287), the nun teacher Shidō, foundress of Tōkeiji, addressed the nuns assembled for the ceremony, standing below the pavilion. She asked them:

'The Buddha who is born this day, where does he come from?'

Her attendant Runkai stepped out, and pointed with one hand to heaven and with the other to the earth.

Then the teacher asked again:

'And when that Buddha who has been born has not yet left this world, where is he then?'

Runkai again pointed with one hand to heaven and with the other to earth.

TEST

When the questions came, about Śākyamuni Buddha before he was born, and again after he was born, Runkai (who became the second teacher at Tōkeiji) pointed at heaven and pointed at earth in the same way each time. Do the two answers, pointing to heaven and pointing to earth in regard to the Buddha before birth, and pointing to heaven and pointing to earth in regard to the Buddha after his birth, have the same meaning, or do they have different meanings? Say how it is!

This became a kōan in Kamakura Zen at the interviews of Ryōdō, the 7th teacher at Tōkeiji.

(Imai's note: An account of Ryōdō, who after many vicissitudes found a teacher in Master Daiei and underwent a long training with him, finally grasped the essence of his teaching and became the 7th teacher at Tōkeiji, is given in the section on the nuns of Eastern Japan, in the commentary to the Sōrinzakki, volume 7.)

No. 83. Tengai's heart-binding

In the fighting in the Gankō era (1331–4), the Nitta forces set fire to Kamakura, and (sparks) from the burning streets carried the fire to fishing villages and mountain hamlets, so that their people were fleeing in all directions before the blaze, crying out with fear. The priests of the Kamakura temples guided and distributed them among the temples, and used the produce of the temple lands to feed the destitute. At the same time there were many relatives of the refugees imprisoned in the caves (used as prisons) who were choking in the smoke and on the verge of dying of suffocation, at which their families were in great distress.

Then Hakuun (namely Butchō, 26th master of Kenchōji), Tengai (namely Shinkaku, 19th master at Enkakuji), Reikō of Jufukuji, and Tengan of Inayama and others organized the laymen and priests, and battered down the gates of the caves, setting free the prisoners, whom they conducted to the various temples.

The officer of prisons protested that these were criminals of violent character, who if not under restraint would disperse and do great damage to the ordinary people. Tengai of Enkakuji laughed and told him, 'However many thousands of criminals there might be, they can be held with merely a single rosary. No need to worry about it.'

Next day he had them brought from all the temples to the great hall at Zenkōji, where he held up his rosary in front of them and said: 'Yesterday we saved you from the raging fire and brought you to safety and gave you food and clothes to relieve your hunger and cold. But as law-breakers, it is proper that you be under restraint. Now with this single rosary I bind your hearts and prohibit you from doing any wrong. You will follow the path ordained for you, and never resort to violence.'

They were impressed by this, and not one of them disobeyed the instructions they were given by the priests and lay officers. After the destruction of the Hōjō Government, many of them became workers on the lands of the various temples. Bairin (37th master at Enkakuji) at the end of a sermon, admonished Hatayama Yoshinori, who was a pupil and an official in charge of prisons:

'Does Your Honour use a long rope to restrain criminals? It will indeed serve to restrain their bodies. But to bind their hearts, one inch of cord is more than enough. In the Genkō fighting, there were criminals – who knows how many hundreds or thousands? – in the great hall of Zenkōji, but Tengai of this temple in one instant bound them all with a single rosary. If Your Honour and the other officers bind the hearts of the wrong-doers, they will respect and obey you, and many will reform and turn to good. If you simply punish them by confining their bodies, certainly the effect will be that no small number will become violently rebellious.'

Hatayama said: 'How is the heart of the law-breaker to be bound?'

The teacher said: 'People have in their inner heart evil-doers – who knows how many hundreds or thousands? – in revolt against the Lord of the heart. If you do not bind them by Zen meditation, and (ultimately) kill them by prajñā wisdom, there will never be true peace there. Now if the officer is asking how he may bind the hearts of others, let him first bind his own heart.'

The pupil said, 'How am I to bind my own heart?'

The teacher said in a loud voice, 'Lord Hatayama!'

'Yes?' said the officer.

The teacher said, 'Bind the asking.'

On these words the pupil understood. He bowed and went out.

TESTS

(1) Say what is your own heart.
(2) Who is it who binds?
(3) How is the binding done? Say!
(4) One's own heart is often astray; how will it bind the heart of another? Say! Bring the proof to show.

This incident became a kōan at the interviews of Bairin, 37th master at Enkakuji.

No. 84.   *The Lanka sūtra of one word*

Kataoka Moritada had studied spells for a long time under a teacher of the Esoteric Shingon sect. Happening to stay overnight in one of the guest rooms at Kenchōji temple, he asked priest Kinkei:

'In the Lanka sūtra spells which are recited by the Zen sect followers, there are many names of the terrible gods invoked by the followers of the outer ways in the heaven of the west (India). What good is it to recite that sort of spell?'

'Don't you know what is said in the sūtra itself?' replied the teacher. 'It says that water drunk by the snake becomes poison, but the water drunk by a cow becomes milk. In the same way, the terrible gods of India, when they come into the heart of a Zen man, become protective divinities for the dharma; so when he recites them, the terrible gods of India become great manifestations of Bodhisattvas to save the world. To recite such spells, what harm is there in that?'

The inquirer said: 'I'm not saying anything about harm. I'm asking what good it is.'

The teacher said: 'Good is in the heart of the reciter; it has nothing to do with saying spells.'

The inquirer said: 'If so, then rather than reciting the long spells of the Lanka sūtra, it would be better to use the short spells of Shingon.'

The teacher replied: 'The recitation of the Lanka spells in our sect had its origin with the Sung master Shinketsu as a propitiatory prayer for relief against plague, but always a Zen man when he recites long spells, is doing so simply as a prop to help the feelings of other people. If for ourselves we recite the Lanka sūtra spell, we do it in just one word. The gateway to the true spell of the Zen sect is the course of the four postures (standing, sitting, lying, going). What need to talk about long or short spells?'

TEST
Say the Lanka spell in just one word.

This incident became a kōan in Kamakura Zen at the interviews of priest Sōen, the 62nd master at Kenchōji.

No. 85.   One law, a thousand words

Hosoi Naotaka, the superintendent of the temple lands, came to the teaching hall at Kenchōji and asked the teacher Hōrin after the sermon:

'If someone doesn't understand the meaning of the sūtras, but still recites them, does he have merit or not?'

The teacher said: 'It's like a man who takes medicine. Even if he doesn't know the principles of a good medicine, still if he takes it, it will do him good. And it's like that with a poison: if he doesn't know that this particular thing is in essence a poison, when he takes it he'll die. Or again, it's like travelling in a ship. Even though one may not know the principles of the construction of a ship, still, if he boards it he will arrive at his destination. Reading the sūtras is like that. Though one may not know the principle of law (dharma), if he recites, and he has faith and he does right conduct, the merit will be without limit.

'These days the autumn is warm, and in the gardens you've got so many things to do. A superintendent of agriculture like you, a layman, why are you concerned with what goes on in the daily services in the temple?'

'If it's not necessary to listen to the principle of the sūtras,' replied the superintendent, 'why is it then that priests, and you yourself, for so many years have been conducting these daily services?'

The teacher said: 'The people at large have very many illnesses, and they go astray from the Way, or they are confused about the Way. It's like providing medicines, or building a boat. We are talking about the arts of doing those things, making up medicines and building boats. The pharmacist and the boatman are specialists in the principles which are the law for their craft. The whole point is that one law is expressed in a thousand words, or ten thousand sayings.'

The superintendent of agriculture said: 'Well, can one then hear this law? How is one to hear it?'

The teacher said: 'The one law comprises warriors, workers on the land, artisans and merchants, all of them. You yourself every day, you are in the gardens and in your digging the ground and your ploughing, in all that there is the great manifestation and the great application of this law. If you don't see it, look down where your feet have been for thirty years!'

TESTS

(1) What is the one law before father and mother were born? Say!

(2) You right now, how do you apply that one law? Say!

(3) You are at the point of death and can't use either hands or feet or nose or mouth, and somebody comes to you and

asks to be taught about the one law. How are you going
to give your sermon? Say!

(4) You have gone to hell on a mission impelled by your
karma, to save the beings there, and now you face these
beings who are screaming in their terrible torments. How
do you preach the one law to them? And how are you
going to save them? Say!

This incident became a kōan in Kamakura Zen at the
interviews of priest Zōkai who was the 17th master at
Kenchōji.

No. 86. *Ku-an's three questions*

Yūki Sukemochi was one of the most arrogant feudal lords,
feared by others for his strong self-will. In the first month of
the twentieth year of Ōei (1413) he came to the Shunkeidō
(the guest temple at Kenchōji), paid his respects to Priest Ku-
an (the preacher at the Gyoku-un hall, and a son of the great
Uesugi family, which dominated this part of Japan for
centuries), and asked about the importance of learning in the
Way.

The priest said: 'First get rid of self-will. If one is infected
with worms in the intestines, he may take in nourishment but
it simply increases the worms, and often he loses his life. With
human nature itself, it is the same. If there is the worm of self-
will in one's breast, though he may take in learning to give
nourishment to his heart, it simply increases the self-will and
is of no use in the Way. The Way of the superior man is,
rather than seeking acclaim for intellectual knowledge, to
strive to increase his virtue.'

The warrior said, 'But without self-will, one could not raise
one's own standing nor bring success to the family.'

The teacher said: 'You have still not released yourself from
self-will. Getting rid of self-will means clearing away the

arrogance from the heart. In ancient times and later on, there have been those who made themselves and their families illustrious as sages and saints, so that their names still remain after a hundred generations. How did they hold pride in their hearts? But if Your Honour believes that self-will is so important, I will put three questions to you, and do you reply to them:

This self – where was it before it put out its head into the world? Right now in the body, where is this self? When the body perishes, where does this self go to?'

The warrior could think of no reply, and took his leave.

TEST
Bring a word for Sukemochi.

This became a kōan in Kamakura Zen in the interviews of Gesō, the 125th master at Kenchōji.

No. 87.   *The sermon of Nun Shidō*

At the Rōhatsu training week of 1304 at Enkakuji, Master Tōkei ('Peach-tree Valley' – the fourth teacher of Enkakuji) gave his formal approval (inka) as a teacher to the nun Shidō, the founder of Tōkeiji. The head monk did not approve of the inka being granted, and asked a question to test her:

'In our line, one who receives the inka gives a discourse on the Rinzairoku classic. Can the nun teacher really brandish the staff of the Dharma in the Dharma-seat?'

She faced him, drew out the ten-inch knife carried by all women of the warrior class, and held it up: 'Certainly a Zen teacher of the line of the patriarch should go up on the high seat and speak on the book. But I am a woman of the warrior line and I should declare our teaching when really face to face with a drawn sword. What book should I need?'

No. 15 The nun Shidō
(International Society for Educational Information, Tokyo)

The head monk said, 'Before father and mother were born, with what then will you declare our teaching?'

The nun closed her eyes for some time. Then she said, 'Do you understand?'

The head monk said in verse:

149

'A wine-gourd has been tipped right up in Peach-tree Valley;
Drunken eyes see ten miles of flowers.'

TESTS

(1) Before father and mother were born, what was the
    sermon? Say!
(2) Listen to the sermon of the nun Shidō.
    These two tests were used from the time of Daisen, the
    17th teacher in Enkakuji itself, but at Tōkeiji two more
    were added in the interviews of the nun teacher Shōtaku:
(3) What is the meaning of the poem made by the head
    monk?
(4) Are its two lines praise or criticism?

No. 88. The Knight patriarch coming from the west

Yamana Morofuyu was a brave warrior of the Ashikagas,
who was transferred from being a naval captain to the
cavalry. For some time after that he trained in Zen at
Enkakuji. One year he came to the Rōhatsu training week in
December, but would not sit in the special meditation hall
reserved for the warriors. Instead he was riding his horse all
day in the mountains. Master Daikyo, the 43rd teacher at
Enkakuji, warned him against this, saying, 'On horseback
your heart will easily be distracted. During the Rōhatsu, sit in
the hall.'

He said: 'Monks are men of Zen sitting, and should
certainly do their meditation in the special Buddha place. But
I am a knight and should practise my meditation on
horseback.'

The teacher said, 'Your Honour was formerly a sea captain,
and now become a knight. The patriarch's coming (from
India to China) on the waves, and the patriarch's coming on
horseback, is the meaning the same or different?'

Morofuyu hesitated.

The teacher snatched the whip and hit him with it, saying, 'Oh, ride away, ride away.'

TEST

Say something for Morofuyu.

This became a kōan in Kamakura Zen with the interviews of master Chintei, the 47th teacher at Enkakuji.

No. 89. *Sadatsune receives the precepts*

In the fourth month of the tenth year of Ōei (1403), the Ajari (high priest) Shinchō of the Ritsu sect set up an ordination platform for a public ceremony, the classical Buddhist rite of Administering the Precepts. Doi Sadatsune went to see it, and asked the Ajari: 'Are the precepts administered to the body, or are they administered to the mind?'

The Ajari said: 'They are administered to both body and mind together.'

Sadatsune said: 'If it is the body to which they are administered, what happens when the four great elements become separated (at death)? And if it is the heart, that is something which when we try to find it, we cannot get hold of it. How can they be administered to something which has no form?'

The Ajari replied: 'Unless one has faith that he is receiving them, they cannot be administered.'

Sadatsune said: 'When we try to find the heart, we cannot get hold of it; how can you say the precepts are administered? Don't you see what is said in the Heart Sūtra, *No eye, nor ear, nose, tongue, body nor mind; no form, sound, smell, taste, touch, nor object of mind.* Then how can precepts ever be administered?'

The Ajari had no answer.

Sadatsune went to Ganmyō, in charge of the bell pagoda at Kenchōji, told him what had happened and put the point to him. He said:

'The essence of the precepts which we teach in our school is that heart, Buddha, and living beings are all three without distinction between them; as all men are endowed with the essence, we do not speak of administering or receiving it. The *application* of the precepts is to perform the great dharma while in the world, and finally to practise it as a monk, and this is man's path. The *form* of the precepts is perfect performance of the classical ceremony. If there is a man in whom the application of them appears clearly, he is revered by the world. Thus the precepts pervade both absolute and provisional truth, and become a way of opening up realization in place of ignorance; they are the dharma which brings peace to the country and happiness to its people.'

Sadatsune said: 'I am not asking about the rights and wrongs of the precepts, but only the truth about the administering and receiving.'

The monk brought this to Hōgai (47th master of Kenchōji), who invited Sadatsune to an interview, and said to him:

'Why should we need many words about administering and receiving the precepts of dharma?'

He stared at him with a penetrating glance, and called in a loud voice:

'Sadatsune!'

'Yes?' answered the warrior.

The teacher said: 'The precepts have been administered.'

At these words, Sadatsune had a realization and said, 'Today the precepts have been completely received.'

TESTS

(1) The heart of man is vast, without shape or form: how then are the precepts to be administered to it?

(2) How was it that Sadatsune received the precepts from what Priest Hōgai said?

This became a Kamakura kōan at the interviews of Chūzan, the 56th master at Kenchōji.

No. 90. *The Great Katzu! of Ryūhō*

In the seventh month of the first year of Kōwa (1381), which was thirty-three years after the death of Hatayama Michichika (who had been in charge of military affairs for the whole Kantō area), a memorial service was held for him. The people assembled at Hōkizan (the Zen temple Chōjuji), and among them Hatayama Sukemichi came in a palanquin. He saluted priest Ryūhō, the 13th master there, and asked him about memorial services.

The teacher told him: 'A memorial service after forty-nine days is laid down in the sūtras. The services after a hundred days, one year, and three years, derive from traditions in China. The thirteenth year and thirty-third year services were inaugurated when the son of Councillor Nobunishi first had these ceremonies performed out of filial devotion for his father. Memorial services after fifty years and a hundred years and so on are performed in the temples of both Japan and China.'

Sukemichi asked: 'If someone makes a vow to perform the ceremony but does not carry it out, will the spirit of the dead suffer?'

The teacher replied: 'The services are to remind the descendants of the virtues of the deceased; as an expression of their devotion, they pray for his welfare. But the pain or happiness of the spirit of the deceased is according to his karma, so the sūtras declare. But it must be said that for a follower of Zen, there is something more apart from this.'

The pupil persisted in asking that the teacher should declare it, and finally the master glared at him and gave a great Katzu! shout, whereupon he swooned and lost consciousness. After

153

some time the teacher gave another shout and Sukemichi revived.

The teacher said: 'Well, how are they, the happiness and pains of the departed? What you have experienced for yourself, you do not need others to tell you.'

The pupil bowed with gratitude and said: 'In all my seventy-two years it is only now that I have come to know the real meaning of the shout which the Zen priest gives before the coffin at the funeral service.'

TESTS

(1) How are they, the happiness and pains of the departed?
(2) This which is before your eyes, kill it and bring it to life.
     Let me see the proof of it.

This incident became a kōan in Kamakura Zen at the interviews of Ichigen, the 115th master at Kenchōji.
(Imai's note: Since to pass this kōan is a question of actually killing and reviving, those whose power in the Way is not fully matured cannot take it up. According to what I have heard from laymen like Tsuchiya Daian and Yamada Ichimisei, in the old days lay students were tested on the kōan by their teachers in Kamakura Zen in this way: Master Keichū would point to a sparrow in the forecourt, and Kōsen to a cicada on a pine tree, and require them to demonstrate their ability. Sekiso would point to a bluebottle in the room, and Shinjō would put before them a worm, so that the power of killing and reviving could be shown clearly. In any case, this is a kōan that cannot be attempted by one who is not like the old warriors of Kamakura in furious energy in the Way.

Says Fukuzan (Imai): according to what I have heard from Tsuchiya and Yamada, the Katzu! in Kamakura Zen is not to be thought of as a matter of killing and reviving a man. I therefore point out that to kill and revive can also be practised by experts in the art of Kiai (concentrating the vital energy with a shout) and it was something known to experts in

Kendō like Miyamoto Musashi and Tsukahara Bokuden. In the Kendō school of Sakuma Shintōsai, no one could be given the Tiger Scroll (attestation that he had mastered the highest secret of the school) unless he could kill and revive a man by a single kiai shout. But ability to kill and revive by a shout is not prized in Zen: the Zen practice of the shout is quite different from that of the warriors. The Zen shout is the spiritual realization of the Diamond King's Sword, which by one shout has to be a means to resolve Ignorance and open up realization. It has to be spiritually effective in changing by a single shout the six paths and the four kinds of birth into Buddhahood. This is the difference between the Zen practice of Katzu! and the kiai shout of the warriors. There have been those who having penetrated to the inner secrets of Kendō fencing, could strike down and then revive by giving a shout. Among them however were many who when themselves confronting the barrier of life and death, failed at that barrier. This was because their art did not aim at the spiritual development of the Diamond King's Sword. It must be realized that the Kamakura Zen practice of the Katzu! did not aim at producing mere ability to strike down and revive irrespective of spiritual experience of the Diamond Sword; the former was in our school no more than the power of Zen realization. It was not the same thing as what the warriors attained, who from the very beginning were training only for striking and reviving. If the latter were the main thing, then a man very ill, whose throat was choked or who could not open his mouth, would not be able to make the shout and so show his skill. In Kamakura Zen, therefore, even warriors who could come to the interview room and demonstrate their ability to kill and revive some creature with a shout, were not allowed to pass the kōan unless they had the spiritual experience of the Diamond Sword. Later generations in Zen have often wrongly supposed that the Kamakura Zen Katzu! was simply a little art of killing and bringing back to life, and I have therefore added this note.)

From ancient times in the Zen world of Eastern Japan, the three kōans, 68, its variant, and this one, were known as the Three Barriers in Kamakura Zen. But in fact if one of them is passed, the other two are merely variations: it is simply that there are different chakugo comments for each of the three.

No. 91. Daiye's verse on 'not'

(Translator's note: The Japanese read a Chinese text by adding inflections to the ideograms, which are without them, and by changing the order of reading the words in order to make up a Japanese sentence. To assist the reader, they developed a system of 'pointing', to indicate the necessary alterations. An example from English would be the terminations put after figures of dates: 2nd means that the digit is in this case to be read not as 'two' but as 'second'. Some Japanese scholars specialized in putting the 'points' into Chinese texts, which were sometimes printed with them to assist Japanese readers.

In the present case, the 'poem' consists of the Chinese character for 'not' repeated twenty times, in four lines of five characters each. As an example, they might be 'pointed':

not-Not; Not 'not-Not'; not 'Not not-Not', and so on. The kōan, on the face of it, was a challenge to the scholar to provide such pointings.)

In the Bunei era (1264–75) the Chinese priest Daitai (Zen master Butsugen, namely Daikyū) came to Kamakura and became the first teacher at Kanpō temple (Jōchiji). The nobleman Hiromaro, when he met the teacher, remarked: 'For some years now I have been engaged in an official capacity in pointing many Chinese texts for use by Japanese. Your Reverence must have brought many such texts from China, and if I should be so fortunate as to be allowed the loan of them, I could put in points. This would surely be of immeasurable benefit to Japanese readers.'

The teacher said: 'What I did bring was the verse which Master Daiye composed on the word 'not' (mu). It runs like this':

> not not not not not
> not not not not not
> not not not not not
> not not not not not

The learned Hiromaro looked at this for a long time, but though it is only a single character, he was unable to put points to it. He made a salutation and departed.

TESTS

(1) Put the points to Daiye's four lines of 'not'.
(2) What does the verse mean? Say!
(3) Add a comment for the first line.
(4) Add a comment for the second line.
(5) Add a comment for the third line.
(6) Add a comment for the fourth line.
(7) Add a comment for the verse as a whole.
(8) How would you apply this verse to life? Bring a comment.
(9) How would you look at Buddhism in the light of this verse? Bring a comment.
(10) What do you yourself understand in regard to this verse? Bring a comment.

This became a kōan in Kamakura Zen in the interviews of Tōri, 16th master at Kenchōji.

No. 92. *Meditation of the energy-sea*

A retired landowner named Sadashige of Awafune (the present-day Ofuna) trained at Kenchōji under Nanzan, the 20th master. Once he was away for a time and when he returned the teacher said, 'You have been ill, Sir, and for some time you have not come to the Zen sitting here. Have you now been able to purify and calm your kikai (energy-sea)?'

Sadashige said, 'Following your holy instruction I have meditated on the kikai and been able to attain purity and calm.'

The teacher said, 'Bring out what you have understood of the meditation and say something on it.'

(1) This my kikai tanden, breast, belly, [down to the] soles of the feet, [is] altogether my original face.

TEST
What nostrils would there be on that face?

(2) This my kikai tanden
[is] altogether this my true home.

TEST
What news would there be from the true home?

(3) This my kikai tanden
[is] altogether this my lotus paradise of consciousness only.

TEST
What pomp would there be in the lotus paradise?

(4) This my kikai tanden
[is] altogether the Amida of my own body.

TEST
What sermon would that Amida be preaching?

This kōan was first given in the interviews of Master Nanzan. *(Note: In the Bushōsōdan record in Zenkōji these are given as four separate meditations. Centuries later, Hakuin refers to them in two works, Oategama and Yasenkanna. The version in 'Yasenkanna' is closest to the one here. The four meditations are identical except that the first one has 'loins, legs, soles of the feet', and in all four the phrase kikai tanden is preceded by the descriptive 'below the navel'. Some of the Chinese expressions are given in a similar Japanese form. Each kōan and its test run on as one sentence. In Oategama there are more changes. The phrase 'loins, legs, soles of the feet' is repeated each time, the order is changed, and there is an extra kōan '. . . altogether this is Jōshū's Mu: what is the truth of the Mu?' In this version the 'my' is omitted before 'original face'. These are small changes and it is clear that Hakuin must derive his kikai tanden method from the Kamakura text, or from a source common to both. – Tr.)*

No. 93. Tōzan's Who's-This?

At the end of the Genkō period (1331–4) there was continuous fighting. People were in peril of their lives, and no one's heart was at rest. The village people began to throng to the temples, where they prayed to be spared from disaster. In various sects there appeared crafty priests, who preyed on the fears of the people by organizing prayer meetings where they sold charms. In these ways they enriched their temples. Many of these clever talkers were active among the people. And some of the Zen laymen began to be caught up in the same ideas, taking to coming into the main hall and praying to be spared, or else to be resigned to whatever might come. In this way they neglected the true Buddha within.

At this time master Nanzan (the 20th teacher at Kenchōji), concerned at the loss of the spirit of Zen, began to give the 'Who's-This?' sermon of Tōzan as a kōan to Zen laymen when he met them. Kuribune was one who worked at it for a long time, and in the end grasped it.

THE WHO'S-THIS? SERMON

Zen master Tōzan (the Chinese master known in Japan as
Goso Hōen) said: Shākya and Maitreya are fine fellows, but
how about Who's-This?

TESTS

(1) What are Shākya and Maitreya?
(2) What is this Who's-This?
(3) What is this 'fellow'?
(4) What am I?
(5) Who is this 'Who's-This?'
(6) Who's-This Shākya, and Maitreya?
(7) What does master Tōzan really mean?
(8) Make a comment of your own on what Tōzan said.

*(Imai's comment: The fact that master Nanzan gave this to
his warrior pupils appears in the Bukedōshinshū (the 17th
volume in the Nirayama copy). It became a kōan at
Kamakura after this teacher.)*

No. 94. *Tanka's Buddha-burning*

*(Translator's note: Tanka was a Chinese Zen master who
died in 824 AD, and was famous for having burnt a wooden
Buddha to make a fire on a very cold winter night, there being
no other fuel. For this he was severely reprimanded by the
superintendent priest of the temple. The latter however found
his own eyebrows falling off, a traditional sign of something
spiritually wrong. There are many pictures of the Buddha-
burning incident, including a most unconventional one by
Fūgai in Japan.)*

Norimasa, an artist training in Zen, was visiting the
Shōgatsuan temple of Kamegayatsu (the pagoda of Jufukuji
temple) when he noticed a scroll depicting Tanka burning the
Buddha. He asked about the meaning of Tanka's Buddha-

burning. Priest Ryōzen, who was in charge of the temple, told him:

'It is as a means to show how the physical form is destroyed, and with that burning to ashes of the wooden Buddha, the true essence stands out.'

The artist said: 'I have heard from you the truth of his Buddha-burning. But – I wonder – what did the temple supervisor do wrong that his eyebrows dropped off when he reproved Tanka so severely?'

The priest said: 'Yes, what would he have done wrong? Do you meditate on it, and penetrate into it.'

TESTS

(1) Why was it that Tanka burnt the Buddha?
(2) Why was it that the temple supervisor's eyebrows dropped off?
(3) Suppose right now there is someone in front of you burning a wooden Buddha, how will *you* meet the situation?

This incident became a kōan in Kamakura Zen at the interviews of Myō-ō, the 45th master at Zenkōji and a teacher of the Ōryū line.

No. 95. *The four Dharma-worlds of a teacup*

On the first day of the series of discourses on the Kegon sūtra, the priest Ryōkan (of the Tsurugaoka Hachiman shrine) came, and asked Seizan (Zen master Bukkan, the 39th master at Kenchōji) for an explanation of the four Dharma-worlds (of Ri the principle, Ji the event, Riji-muge where principle and event are interpenetrating, and Jijimuge where events interpenetrate each other).

The teacher said: 'To explain the four Dharma-worlds should not need a lot of chatter.'

He filled a white cup with tea, drank it up, and smashed the cup to pieces right in front of the priest, saying, 'Have you got it?'

The priest said: 'Thanks to your here-and-now teaching, I have penetrated right into the realms of Principle and Event.'

TESTS

(1) What is the truth of the four Dharma-worlds of the teacup? Say!

(2) Show the four Dharma-worlds in yourself.

This incident became a kōan in Kamakura Zen at the interviews at Etsugan, the 75th master at Kenchōji.

No. 96. *The diamond realm*

In the twentieth year of Ōei (1313), on the evening of the seventh day of the Rōhatsu (December training week), Suketaka Nyūdō, a Zen layman training there, crept into the Buddha hall at Kenchōji and stole the delicacies from the altar to make up for the poor food. However, the monk in charge of the hall happened to come back, and caught him. He said to him: 'According to the Rōhatsu rules, this week is the strictest time of the whole year. For you to steal the food from the Buddha hall at a time like this is no small crime. But I will put a question to you, and if you can answer, I will let you off.'

Suketaka replied, 'Out with it then.'

The monk said, 'What is it, your taking the food like this?'

The other answered, 'The universal body (dharma-kāya) eats the cakes, the cakes eat the dharma-kāya.'

The monk said, 'Is the difference between you and the universal body large or small?'

Suketaka said, 'The taste of the salt in the water: the transparent glue which holds the colours of the paints.'

The monk said, 'What is that supposed to mean?'

Suketaka said, 'A gust of wind – the more you try to paint it the more you fail.'

The monk said, 'Let's try to paint it.'

The samurai then said, 'The diamond realm.'

The monk said, 'The diamond realm – what's that?'

Suketaka replied, 'Going into the fire it does not burn; going into the water, it does not drown.'

The monk of the hall said, 'Let us try a test on you.' He took a bundle of incense sticks *(at that period it would be 200 sticks – Imai)*, set them alight and put them on the other's head. The warrior leapt up and ran out towards the training hall; he tripped and fell into the big Sleeping Dragon well at the bottom of the steps.

The monk put the lid on the well and cried, 'Just now you were saying that in fire it does not burn, and in water it does not drown. Now say quick, what is the diamond realm!'

Suketaka could find no reply.

TESTS

(1) Say something of your own on the diamond realm in the fire.

(2) Say something of your own on the diamond realm in the water.

(3) Say something of your own on the diamond realm on the edge of a sword.

(4) Say something of your own on the diamond realm in the wineshop and in the brothel.

(5) Say something on the diamond realm on the thirtieth day of Rōhatsu (after death).

(6) Say something on the diamond realm in the screams of hell.

(7) That thieving man said, 'The dharma-body eats the cakes; the cakes eat the dharma-body.' What should these words really mean?

(8) Again he said, 'A gust of wind – the more you try to paint

it the more you fail.' What is the essential principle in
this?

This first became a kōan in Kamakura Zen at the interviews
of Daiju, the 157th teacher at Kenchōji.

No. 97.   *Meeting after death*

In the second year of Eitoku (1382), on the 25th day of the
11th month Daigaku, the 46th master at Enkakuji, was lying
ill, and knowing it was the eve of his departure (he died the
next day) had a message sent to the lay pupils who had been
with him a long time. One of them, Masumitsu of Namerikawa,
came straight away and stood in attendance at the side of the
master's bed (on the ground).

He said: 'It is only four years till the master reaches the
auspicious classical span of eighty-eight years; that should not
have been long to wait to leave this world of Saṃsāra. But
now having just caught this fever that is going round, there is
only a little of the month left to think about it; so I came to see
the old master for the crisis.'

He stepped forward quickly and kicked the wooden pillow.

The teacher tested him: 'The old priest dies, the old official
dies. When they have both been cremated and reduced to
ashes, when is the time and where is the place that they meet
again?'

The warrior made a comment.

The teacher nodded.

TESTS

(1) What does it mean, this meeting again after death?
(2) What was Masumitsu's comment? Say!

This became a kōan at Kamakura at the interviews of Kyūge,
the 95th master at Enkakuji.

No. 98.   *Maudgalyāyana's mother*

In the eighth month of the first year of Bunna (1352), on the day of the airing of the temple scrolls at Jufukuji, a high official who also trained at Zen came to see them, and was greatly impressed with a Sung dynasty picture of Maudgalyāyana's mother falling into hell.

He said to the monk in charge: 'I have heard in the Zen priests' sermons the phrase, *When a son renounces home, the ancestors for nine generations attain a birth in heaven.* So what is happening here? How is it that the mother of Maudgalyāyana, one of the Buddha's ten great disciples, falls into hell?'

The monk said, 'The meaning of a Zen phrase must not be sought in the words as they stand. When the Zen priests say *a son*, I myself am the son; and *renounces home* means that he renounces the whole world. *Nine generations of ancestors* means the nine worlds out of the ten, and *birth in heaven* means to ascend to the Buddha world, the tenth. So *When a son renounces home, nine generations of ancestors attain heaven* means that this son who is I has been wandering lost in the nine worlds, but when he leaves the worlds of distinctions, the nine worlds become the heaven of Vairocana (the Buddha world), and all ten worlds attain fulfilment.'

The visitor said, 'I have listened to your Zen explanation. But even so, how was it that when for some reason his mother was falling into hell, Maudgalyāyana, first of the disciples in supernatural powers, was unable to help her?'

The monk said, 'Ask someone else.'

TESTS

(1) Say something for the monk.
(2) If someone comes and asks you what the words, about the son renouncing home and the ancestors being born in

heaven, really mean, how will you make a response? (Those who use what the monk said will not be passed by the teacher.)

This became a kōan in Kamakura at the interviews of master Kendō, the 70th teacher at Zenkōji.

(Note by Imai Fukuzan: The words, One youth renounces home and nine generations of ancestors are born in heaven *come in the 'comments' to some of the Kamakura kōans. This is then being used in a different sense from that of the ordinary Zen understanding of it. The ancient phrase traditionally ascribed to Ōbaku is quite different.*

In answering the second test, it is no use trying to make something of what the monk said. One will have had to pass through one of the basic kōans first before he can produce anything.)

No. 99.   *The iron bar of 10,000 miles*

During the campaign of 1331, Wada Tsunetō was an officer at the Kobukuro camp of the Nitta forces, and also a student of Zen. He came on horseback to the Sōgon gate of Enkakuji and sought to enter, but the warden at the gate barred his way, saying 'Do you dismount.'

He refused, whereupon the warden drew his sword and said, 'In our Zen, there is a saying about racing one's horse along the edge of a sword. If the gallant officer can race his horse along the edge of my sword, I will agree that he should enter the gate.'

The warrior said: 'Before I race along it, what is that sword of yours made of?'

The warden said: 'An iron bar of 10,000 miles.'

TESTS
(1) What does it mean, this 10,000 miles?

(2) What is this iron bar?

(3) How can you get 10,000 miles with an iron bar?

(4) Find two phrases from the Heart Sūtra for the iron bar of 10,000 miles.

This became a kōan in Kamakura Zen at the interviews of Kizan, the 35th master at Enkakuji.

No. 100.   Freeing the ghost

In the first year of Einin (1293) Hirotada was taking as a kōan the four phrases of the Diamond sūtra:

> If as a form he would see me,
>> Or by sound or word would seek me,
> This one on the wrong path
>> Cannot see the Buddha.

He could not penetrate into it. He was sitting in meditation in the cave called Snowgate, which is one of the three near the Tosotsuryō, the tomb of the founder of Kenchōji. While he was unaware of anything in his samādhi, the ground opened and the timbers and stones of the building collapsed into the fissure, burying him. That night the apparition of Hirotada was seen before the hall of the founder, repeating *Cannot see the Buddha, cannot see the Buddha* without ceasing. The monk Mori Sōkei, who had the position of jishinban, confronted the ghost and shouted one question, at which it suddenly vanished and never showed itself again.

(Imai's note: In 1293 there was a great earthquake at Kamakura, during which the ground opened, bringing down buildings and killing many people. This was the occasion for the first of the great fires at Kenchōji.)

TESTS

(1) Why did the head monk have to ask the question? Say!

167

(2) What is the connection between the question and *Cannot see the Buddha*? Say!

(3) What did Hirotada's ghost realize that cleared the illusion and opened up realization? Say!

(4) If you yourself come face to face with a ghost, what will you say to free it?

Variation No. 100. Freeing the ghost

In the seventh year of the Ōan era (1374), Yorihisa went into a meditation retreat in the Enmei pavilion on Deer Mountain, outside the mountain gate of Enkakuji. His meditation was on the phrases of the Kegon sūtra:

If one would know all the Buddhas of the three worlds,
> Let him see the nature of the dharma, that all is the creation
> of mind alone

but he had not come to know the Buddhas of the three worlds. While he was sunk in meditation, it happened that the place caught fire, but he was not aware when the roof caught alight, and perished in the flames. That night the ghost of Yorihisa appeared in front of the temple gate intoning again and again *All the Buddhas of the three worlds, all the Buddhas of the three worlds*. The monk in charge of the temple gate reported this to the monks' hall, and Karashigawa Sōryū, who held the office of tantō, went to meet the ghost. He gave a great shout 'Namu Yorihisa Butsu!' (Reverence to Buddha Yorihisa!) and the apparition vanished abruptly and never appeared again.

TESTS

(1) Where are all the Buddhas of the three worlds? Say!

(2) What is the nature of the dharma-world like? Say!

(3) Bring the proof of 'mind-alone'.

(4) What is this about dharma-world nature being the creation of mind alone?

(5) The question which the monk at Kenchōji shouted with a Katzu! and the 'reverence to Buddha Yorihisa' of the Enkakuji head monk – are these ultimately the same thing or not? Explain!

(6) Right now in front of you is the ghost of Minamoto Yoshitsune. Set him free quickly, and show me the proof.

These incidents began to be set as kōans in the interviews of Daiin, the 158th teacher at Kenchōji.

INDEX OF
CHINESE CHARACTERS

This index gives the Chinese characters, some of them not now current, for the less familiar names and technical terms. In a few cases Imai has indicated an unusual reading, and these readings are followed here.

The E and K following the names stand for Enkakuji and Kenchōji respectively; the incumbency was often short, sometimes just two or three years.